Tom Thomson's Shack

Other books by Harold Rhenisch

TOM
THOMSON'S
SHACK

Harold Rhenisch

NEW STAR BOOKS
VANCOUVER
2000

New Star Books Ltd.
107 - 3477 Commercial Street
Vancouver, BC V5N 4E8
www.NewStarBooks.com

Cover designed by The Cardigan Press
Typeset by New Star Books
Printed & bound in Canada by Transcontinental Printing & Graphics
1 2 3 4 5 04 03 02 01 00

Publication of this work is made possible by grants from the Canada
Council, the British Columbia Arts Council, and the Department of
Canadian Heritage Book Publishing Industry Development Program.

Canadä

Le Conseil des Arts | The Canada Council
du Canada | for the Arts

CANADIAN CATALOGUING IN PUBLICATION DATA

Rhenisch, Harold, 1958-
Tom Thomson's shack

ISBN 0-921586-75-2

1. Rhenisch, Harold, 1958- — Journeys — Ontario. 2. Ontario —
Description and travel. I. Title.
PS8585.H54Z53 2000   C814'.54   C00-910253-1
PR9199.3.RR6RZ475 2000

for Heather and Maria

I went to war,
so that my son could be a farmer,
so that his son could be a poet.

THOMAS JEFFERSON

Look again at this country.
It is not as you thought it was.

AL PURDY

And God think should be land.
And if it was land, there should be people in the land.
Be better.

HARRY ROBINSON

I ate pork medallions for Thanksgiving dinner with a banker from Toronto. If we didn't live on opposite sides of the country, we could easily have become good friends. I would have liked that. It wouldn't have been a friendship based on mutual understanding and love, mind you; we wouldn't have got together in the garage and made wine in the fall while the horses watched us patiently from the hill and sparrows flitted through the purple leaves of the pear tree out the door. It would have been a friendship based on shared intellectual excitement and contrasting ideas.

I was the guest of Heather and Maria, my publishers at Wolsak & Wynn. Together we were promoting a book of my poems, *Iodine*. Heather's car was always breaking down on our way to and from engagements. We had to continually change our plans. Maria was always tired, for I was living in a different time zone and kept her up very late, night after night. Despite these limitations, however, Heather and Maria managed to show me Canada. What a place! I had never seen anything quite like it before, even though I have CANADA stamped on my passport. The discovery of that distant country is this book – the act of turning an antique dressing table over and looking at the label on the bottom, yellow with age: *Winnebago*. So that's what they made before they got into rolling stock and houses that just won't stay still: bedroom furniture; someplace to lie down and sleep, and dream, and make love.

I have tried to set down the tastes, smells, memories, and dislocating sense of strangeness and joy, of unreality become real, that were Toronto to me. I have not written a travel brochure and have steered clear of the Victorian boosterism that pads out the Sunday edition of the *Vancouver Sun*, sandwiched between ads for cruise lines and charts giving the worth of the holiday dollar – obviously something different from the one we use every day. This is not that kind of book. This is a book of the forest where I live and of the farms which brought me to it, told in the conversational style of an orchardist's coffee breaks. This is also a book of a city past the end of the earth, a city at the end of time – a strange place, full of paradoxes and visual tricks. The trip there knocked me off centre. That is a good thing in itself, but the trip also gave me more than I had ever dreamed of: I made good friends in a strange land, I tasted a Golden Russet apple – at last – and I got out to Kleinburg to see the Group of Seven. There under the green maples that simply refused to turn red, despite all of Maria's passionate urging and begging and laughter and cajoling, I saw Tom Thomson's shack. It has been eighty years since Tom died. The shack has been empty for a long time. It is time we moved in.

Harold Rhenisch
October 1999
108 Mile Ranch
British Columbia

I

THE FIRST DAYS

OF HISTORY

The country I live in is not on any map. It's a big country, with lots of room to travel. You can make your own way here. Sure, there are old colonial maps, with the names of a few fur-trading posts and the biggest rivers. Land surveyors and chambers of commerce have *their* maps, but they aren't maps of the earth. In the earth, ponderosa pines are not trees but ancient, orange-barked creatures rooted in red volcanic soil, staring with the patience of centuries down hillsides of speargrass and cacti to water – such as the black shale canyon of Barcelo Creek, or Coyote's home, the rushing silver current of the Nicola River.

The Nicola empties into the Thompson at Spences Bridge. With its acacia-shaded motel, three gas stations (two boarded up), and tumble mustard growing between sun-faded houses, Spences Bridge is nothing. The town is completely engulfed by the silence of the earth, the bighorn sheep that drift across the highway in sagebrush-coloured clouds, the purple cliffs, the thin willows lining the gravel bars. The traffic that passes through Spences Bridge on the week-long haul from Toronto to Vancouver moves through this silence at high speed. As you stand at the roadside and watch the roaring trucks and cars, the wind that kicks up behind them scatters fine sand in your eyes – history, moving by. And away: after the whine of the tires settles, after the screeching of the trains, the wild, wheatgrass wind blows in the deep mountain valley, with the rising and sinking of the earth to the sun. It never stops.

I live two hours north of Spences Bridge on the Cariboo Plateau, an old volcanic plain in the centre of British Columbia, a land of pine forests, lakes, and rolling hills, rimmed by tall white-and-blue mountains of glaciers and wolves. In this high country of volatile, ever-changing weather, my house lies at an altitude of nine hundred metres. In the summer the land burns up with heat and the air is often thick for days on end with the smoke of fires. In winter the sky lies close upon the land and the air is so cold and clear it seems something you can grasp. When the temperature drops below minus forty, the whole world goes absolutely still and the stars tremble above the black night house.

I took a crooked path to the plateau. In 1975, while my friends moved to the Cariboo, eager to work on green-chains and to drive Dusters and Mustangs, I left my small farming valley, which I hated, to enter the modern world, which I loved. I think I must have been reading too much Beat poetry, for that was the year I had thought that the most beautiful thing in the world was to sit in an all-night cafe in Victoria with a blue toque pulled down over my long, greasy, yellow hair and eat grilled cheese sandwiches and drink coffee, while cars and people, blurred and beautiful, hooted and slowly streamed past – at 4 a.m. We were all a part of a dance. Well, it was beautiful, even if it was a trance induced by caffeine and fatigue. My friends were probably pretty tired stacking lumber up on the greenchain, too, but for better or for worse they had never read any Beat poetry. I thought it was a terrible shame.

A year later, however, the huge, spreading ocean sunsets in Victoria drove me away. They came in low over the roofs and in long, flaming, liquid rivers between the houses and down the streets. The black, leafless spring trees caught up in them and streamed through the windows, filling the rooms of my apartment with branches. I walked through the trees, out into the sunroom, and stood in the clear air. As the red light of the dying sun bloomed higher and higher into the clouds, I realized that everything I was being taught in university, everything about the barbiturate existential angst of the French philosopher-novelists Camus and Sartre, everything about the displacement of modern man and his longing to be part again of a complete world in which all his desires were balanced, were for me an affectation: I had such a culture and such a home, although I had renounced it. By the time the February rains hit town, the whole attempt of world literature and philosophy left me feeling like I was standing at the bottom of a seamless stone wall three hundred metres high and vanishing into fog. I returned to the Interior and my valley, the Similkameen. There was work to be done. There was history to be written.

On the first day of history, Anna Brown's kids burned her on top of a pile of applewood on her front lawn. It was a hot, windy afternoon in peach season. The sky was thin and blue. Years before, Anna had picked those kids up and fled Ontario for the land – in which I lived. To be perfectly honest, to call Anna's overgrown field of couchgrass and mustard a lawn requires strong religious faith. To say that Anna was burned requires an acceptance that what we think we're going to do has the same force as what we actually get done in the end: a more delicate point. That day in 1979, Anna was toasted, roasted, her hair swept through town in a white cloud, and she was finally buried, almost intact, after a visit from a distraught health nurse. After that came history; after that I went in the opposite direction. When Maria phoned in 1994 to ask if I would come to Toronto to read from my new book of poems, *Iodine*, a celebratory book about farmers, Briggs & Stratton engines, and God, I said "Yes!" I was excited. After fifteen years, I was finally taking the modern world of the land *back* to the city, to see what it could find and to find out what it could give.

In Toronto, Kim Maltman, the nuclear physicist and poet, has been fiddling with words and has discovered that "civilization" is dead – all its ideas, philosophy, art, beauty, and culture no longer jack it up: beauty just doesn't power the machine any more; it might still be present, but it is just a shell, and the stuff that is inside it, cogs and wheels, or a dumpster overflowing with cardboard and gyproc, isn't that pretty at all.

Kim needs to get out of town.

Tom Godin got out of town. "I'm tired of painting birds," he says. He lives in a shack without a phone, out at Buffalo Creek. Tom comes from Kim and Anna's country as well, but from a trapper's cabin in the bush, not from downtown. For tourists he used to paint detailed pictures of birds, and ink drawings of bears and moose on the white underfaces of fungi that grow on the north sides of trees in the Cariboo. He's given that up. "I'm tired of painting nouns! You can paint so every rib of every feather is perfect, but once you've done that, what have you done? You haven't painted a bird! When I see a bird I feel something alive that's not there when I paint it, and it's the reason I painted it. We share this planet, but what a bear or a moose thinks is something we'll never know. I love crows! I've watched them for a long time. I can look at a crow and not see it. It is just black. I can see the space where it is, but I can't see the crow." He lowers his voice. "I don't think they fly at all. They levitate. They get you distracted with their laughing and their wing flapping, and when you're all caught up in that they just lift off the ground, easy as can be. Then they drop down again before you notice what they've done. Then they laugh at you. They make it look so easy. I don't want to paint nouns. I want to paint verbs."

Last winter, when the starlight turned to forty below and blew in big dry drifts over the abandoned and crumbling cement plant at the main intersection in 100 Mile House, Tom Godin's geese hung in the art gallery next door, above the tire shop. It was a show about angels. Tom rose to the challenge: he painted a flock of migrating Canada geese, necks outstretched, with whimsical, Sufistic expressions. An angel flew among them, like a siren on the prow of a pirate ship, robes flowing out behind her, eyes closed in rapture and peace. It was going to be the cover to this book. You had to *love* those geese. They *knew*.

"Oh, *that*!" laughed Tom in the spring while the loons were out herding fish into the shallow water, and the crows were stealing goose eggs. "I painted over it. It served its purpose. I needed the canvas. I can't *work* anymore. I'm finished with that. I have all I need. People say, 'Why don't you get a job?' But what for? I couldn't do that. They think I'm being lazy. 'You just don't get it,' I say to them. 'I'm *unemployable*.' I'm serious. I have all I want for entertainment. I have a lawn chair to sit in in the evening. I have a bird feeder. The cat's not dead yet. *That's* luxury!" Behind him shine the self-portraits of the artists of the town: pastels, watercolours, pen and inks. On the floor is Tom's: an old, dowelled wooden chair, its front legs sitting in a pair of worn workboots, the back legs in a pair of leather work gloves, black on the palms from painting the rest of the stuff. On the chair is a chimney cap, painted black. That's Tom. Well ... maybe. In front of the chair is a "wood" stove: a black-painted cast-iron shell jammed over a bolt of firewood. Behind that is a firescreen: black. Splashed on the floor from the chair legs, around the stove, and up over the screen are shreds of a flag – the red bits, a kind of human shape. That's Tom: a fire, burnt away, leaving this record of its ignition. But it isn't the wood that's burnt: we're talking a different kind of fire here. "I wanted to point out," he says. "We shouldn't be aiming for photography, as if in the end that is the vision that is 'real.'" He tried to sell it for $650. No takers. Good thing, probably: that barely covers the cost of a new woodstove, let alone the chair, the boots, and the gloves. Art is expensive.

Beauty has not vanished from art or life. There are, for instance, wild horses west of my house, on the Chilcotin Plateau. Hunters set snare traps for them, fifty miles from the nearest ranch. Timber cruisers flit through the forests in the winter on their snowmobiles and almost lose their heads to the wires. There might be as many as a hundred and fifty horses running free, no more than that. The horses are snared, shot, chopped up with chainsaws, thrown in the back of pickups, and driven the four hours to Williams Lake, where each one is worth four hundred and fifty bucks: pet food. The law states that only domestic and native animal populations warrant protection. Wild horses are neither. Besides, cattle could eat that grass. It is those horses we identify with, though, running free – not the culture that harvests them as an expression of its freedom. They are who we are.

In the spring here in the Cariboo, the green sky flares like a giant leaf above grey hills. The loons ride the water like hand-built wooden boats: steady, slow, and strong. In a storm they are always there, in the green of shallow water, riding the whitecaps and facing into the cold wind, a hundred yards off the reedbeds, completely alone and unmoving.

It is not a human world.

Peter works for the Ministry of Lands in Kamloops, drafting proposals for land-sharing with the Shuswap Nation. "By definition," he said to me, long before he'd ever even thought about treaty negotiations, "a society must exclude its writers and work against them as much as possible, and continually find ways to exclude them. In the end, a few writers will survive, *despite* society, and will then receive society's highest honours. It has to be that way." He didn't say why. Perhaps it was Plato's old attempt to cleanse cities of unlegislated thought. Plato banished poets from his city of soldiers and philosopher kings, after all, not because they were people of low worth and dubious morals, but because no matter what they had to say, and no matter how profound and vital it was – and Plato admitted it was both – when questioned on it, they could not say what they did or did not know, what their poems meant, or how that related to a philosophical discussion. That made them uncontrollable and dangerous: they could, logically, never be part of the city.

Not knowing anything about definitions of citizenship, a rufous hummingbird, one of the old ones of this earth completely clad in polished copper, uses a tall, thin, crooked twig of the willow bush along the path before my house as a perch. He is a small, copper stain against the lapis blue of the lake. Then suddenly he is gone – so small against the intense reflection of the sky behind him that he slips between the weave of the light: appearing instantly, disappearing instantly.

F ortunately, there is more than one kind of city. In the slow, rolling sea of forest stretching up from Horse Lake, there is a single column of basalt, treeless, and capped with a microwave tower and a radio transmission station – like the CN Tower or an aluminum marker on a blown jack-pine stump, where someone had come once and staked a claim for a silver mine.

I climbed Lone Butte one spring day, when the tiger lilies were golden in the pine forests at its base. A few balsam roots burned like miniature suns on the scree, and lush purple flowers grew on the hexagonal chimneys of the rock, their scent streaming into the wind and off over the highway below. The view from the butte was magnificent. All the houses and farms of the South Cariboo had completely dis-appeared, swallowed by the crowns of the trees growing among them. I was on the mast of a ship, looking over a vast green sea in storm. The radio tower was anchored with long cables bolted deep into the rock, and the microwave tower loomed up beside me, hard and metallic and motionless, as if it had come from a different universe. The butte itself was carpeted thickly with flowers – low-growing, requiring little soil, and able to survive in the wind that flares without pause across the stone. The entire plateau was drenched with flowers, of course, but these flowers were different, more fragile, more rare, and vastly more varied. The reason for the difference struck me immediately: on that small space there are no cows. In fact, on the butte, there have never been any cows. I looked out over the sea of trees again, the height making me feel weightless, as if any gust of wind could tear me over the edge. I thought of all the cattle out there on the plateau, lying with their sisters and calves in the trampled shade around mud holes, stomping under the trees as far as I could see, year after year eating the first leaves of the spring flowers until only the toughest few were left. That afternoon, with the microwave signals of Toronto stockbrokers passing through me on their way to the stockbrokers of Vancouver and the currency traders of Hong Kong, I realized that I have never walked in a forest that has not been culturally altered by cattle. "Forest" is simply the wrong word. We are living in a city for cows.

Gail Morrison likes to see cows under the trees. She ranches at 112 Mile along the old Cariboo Wagon Road and sells gravel on the side. 112 Mile used to be a thriving roadhouse a few days' journey north of Lillooet, a windy staging post on the Fraser River. The 112 is not thriving anymore. Gail grew up there during the Depression – not the Depression of the 1930s, which knocked the prairies and the cities for a loop and entered the history books, when long lines of unemployed young men rode the rails from one side of the country to the other, clinging to the tops of boxcars as the soot rolled over them, but the other Depression, the one that started with the collapse of the Gold Rush in the 1890s and continued right on through until the 1960s, when loggers moved into 100 Mile House and Williams Lake and the trees started to fall.

Gail takes the long view. In the Depression she grew up in, the only food you had for the winter was what you canned yourself in July and August. In those days, ranches floated in the grasslands of the Interior like farms in the veldt of South Africa, cut apart from all civilization, separated by miles of wilderness, in which were scattered a few fishing and hunting lodges. Times have changed. The wilderness lodges are now completely surrounded by lakefront subdivisions, and a third of the Monical Ranch between 103 and 112 Mile houses three thousand people. This last great land grab before the introduction of the Agricultural Land Reserve in 1974 was the dream of Henry Block. Originally, it was to cover the entire 15,000-acre ranch with holiday cabins, linked by a network of trails to a main lodge, with horse rides, tennis, swimming, and golf. The centrepiece of the project was a religious garden, with statuary imported from Italy, carved in the likeness of Henry Block (for Jesus and his friends) and his girlfriend (for Mary and hers). When the land freeze came in, Block gave up in disgust and sold two thirds of the land back to Monical, but while it lasted it was a splash. Prospective buyers received a free flight to Block's own airport in the Cariboo. Block had an office set up in an old Safeway building in Vancouver. You just had to drop in and you were on your way.

"It was the best cattle land in the Cariboo," says Gail, who ranches now on the northern border of the subdivision. "It should never have been sold, and it should all be made ranchland again."

Gail is an elegant woman, and when she speaks she speaks with conviction. All round the southern rim of the plateau, on the vast benches lining the Thompson River and high above the Fraser at Pavilion and Lillooet, where the river is deep in a gorge and the land falls off on both sides into open, dizzying space – where the Coast Mountains rise in blue ranges to the west, each a deeper blue than the last, their glaciers glinting against a searing sky – huge tracts of hay land have been taken out of alfalfa to produce ginseng. It is grown under black shadecloth, in carefully prepared sawdust beds, and nursed along with liberal doses of fungicide. Government money is involved. The Toronto Stock Exchange is in it up to the eyeballs. The ranchers are furious.

Y ou know, I'd like to walk in past the PRIVATE PROP-
ERTY and ABSOLUTELY NO TRESPASSING signs and
through the long avenues of shadecloth, cables, and poisoned
pine sawdust to the Thompson River, the platinum flash of a
fish, among pines whose every needle glows – fibre optic glass
– with the sun. As the blue jays and coveys of California quail
burst out of the Oregon grape and chokecherries, I'd like to
throw rocks from the shore into the current, trying to hit that
point where the water curls back and touches itself in a back
eddy, where the river draining the sky down among us is
absolutely still and the fish come tenderly, floating up, but
which is so small it is difficult to hit as it moves. As the man
who manages this ginseng consortium, with the big billboards along the highway – PACIFIC GINSENG, CANADA'S
MOST PROFITABLE AGRICULTURAL CROP, FOR INVESTMENT
OPPORTUNITIES PHONE DUSTY OR LARISSA – came up in his
pickup and asked me what I was doing on his land – His
Land! God, you gotta hug the guy – I would stand under the
roaring white light of the pine trees and look up at him,
framed there against the one eye of the sky, and climb up to
him. I'd take my time scrambling up the gravel of the bank,
then tell him quietly how in 1971 when the ex-mayor of Penticton, or a priest, or the fire chief, or simply anyone who
wanted to, stopped outside our 115-acre asparagus field, we
would wait until they were out in the middle, picking the
spears; then we would let the air out of all their tires and
drive away, without speaking to them. I'd even tell him how
we had a deal with the gas station a mile down the road to
rent them a hand pump for $5, and how now the asparagus is
all gone, as is the farm, for that matter: despite all our efforts
– or because of them – bankruptcy came. I don't think he
would understand, though. I think he would actually tell me

to get off before he called the cops, although it would probably be better for both of us if he sat down with me on the litter of pine needles and threw rocks into the white throat of the current. The river could make a small mouth for each one of them and swallow them whole, like raindrops.

If my father came along too, he could tell him about that time he drove down the gravel road to the Columbia River outside of Richland, Washington, because he likes to drive down gravel roads just to see what is at the other end, and how when he was down there by the water and the dead, abandoned orchards, with thigh-high grass between the trees, with a derelict town there, along the silver shore, he saw tanks and jeeps coming for him down the hill. He cleared out from the iodine-poisoned soil of the Hanford Nuclear Reservation fast, shaking with fear, because he knew an awful lot about tanks and guns, and he was angry that a government could do that to fruit trees. Maybe we each could sit on either side of the ginseng man and tell him how we hired an old guy with white hair and a double-barrelled shotgun to stay up all night and patrol the ten-pound cabbages at Siberian Flats along the Keremeos Bypass Road so no one stole them, cabbages which we finally plowed under because no one wanted them, which rotted and stank up the whole valley for months, how the Sikhs planted peaches there, with their own dream of owning land, there where the cold air pours out of Apex and the Nickel Plate, and picked two crops in ten years before the cold finally killed the trees.

He might not listen, but there with the river spread out below us and the blue jay light glancing off the cut faces of the water as it reflected the shape of the stones below, it would be good for us, I think, to talk like that, about what concerns us deeply, namely, who has a right to name this land, and how, especially, should it be done?

It is a matter of some debate. At Gustafsen Lake, forty-five minutes west of my house, mountain bluebirds and purple-backed martens flit between the aspen trees, and the lily pads float on the still green water that seems to be cut of stone – so smooth and clean that the sky, the clouds, and the trees exist in a thin film of light, like oil, on the surface. In 1995 a group of Shuswap sun dancers, who wanted to claim that beauty back from the rancher who owned it, started shooting. It took the RCMP, the army, SWAT teams, antipersonnel mines, ten million dollars, and dozens of news reporters to haul the Shuswap off to jail. Ironically, the owner, Lyle James, had been willing to share the land. Things only broke down when the sun dancers refused to accept his primary ownership. It was hopeless. During the standoff, Shuswap women shopping at Safeway in 100 Mile House, buying flour and Kraft Dinner and cereal and carrots, would suddenly be accosted by middle-aged men, their hands extended, a finger pointed forward like a gun.

"Shot any white guys lately?" the men would ask, and then pass by. We are living in a B movie.

I tried to interest the 100 Mile theatre group, the Cariboo Random Players, in producing a play about the Gustafsen Lake standoff. I pitched it as a period treatment of Romeo and Juliet: instead of a struggle between two noble houses, the Montagues and Capulets, damning the young lovers to death, it would be a fight between the RCMP and the Shuswap. What made the idea especially appealing was that the RCMP media spokesman for the event was Staff Sergeant Peter Montague. I thought it was pretty much on the mark. The theatre group wanted dinner theatre, a murder mystery, or *Hello Dolly!*

Gus knows about the business of drawing lines on topographical maps. He ranches at Horse Lake and is the Cariboo representative on the Agricultural Land Reserve board. That puts him in brotherhood with Peter in Kamloops, managing the Indian Reserve system, except Gus likes art and loves to read newspapers from the Coast – the foreign press. There's a stack of old *Vancouver Suns* a yard high beside his worn overstuffed chair. For a pole lamp he has rigged a trouble light to the top of a two-inch-thick flexible aluminum conduit. Old plastic toys hang from the ceiling. He's been shopping at the dump again! Books are stacked high on top of the fridge, and a rubber chicken and a hundred other things are piled up on what was once the dining table. Gus's rooms have a quiet dignity, though. On the wall facing you as you step in hovers an Apache woman by George Littlechild. Her face is coloured in lush swirls of gold and red paint, every colour laid in pure and thick with the tip of George's finger and with brushes of owl and magpie feathers and sweetgrass, and allowed to dry in pools. Facing her from above the overstuffed chair are the green seas of Jack Shadbolt's *Winter Sun Trap*: an ingenious construction of I-beams, baling wire, and scrap lumber set up in desperation to catch the low winter sun as it hangs directly above the horizon, an unmatched and unmatchable seriousness granted to it by modulations of green, black, and a yellow just a grassblade off from yellow. This piece of high art is right at home here.

"Are all ranchhouses in the Cariboo decorated like this?" I ask Gus.

He grins, crookedly. "No." He lets the word trail out, slowly. "Maybe a calendar with a picture of a New Holland baler or something!"

"We all have our coping mechanisms," he adds. We step out into the black and starlit Cariboo night. A green leaf-flicker, trout-nose flare of the northern lights sweeps over the hills in a rough and erratic static.

Raised on the land, yet educated for cities, Gus's and my generation could not cope and left for Calgary, Vancouver, Toronto, Boston, Ottawa, Lausanne, Cincinnati: you name it. Our lives were pushed underground, until there was only the silence. We ran.

Gus and I, however, came back, as few of us came back, to climb the mountains and to see the green waves of the land roll like the sea and break against the ridges and peaks and starlight like foam. We have had to face the fact that our perceptions and passions, here, have still not seen words. We're still out in the mud of the farmyard with a bucket on the front of the tractor, a hydraulic hose that will not couple, and a hammer, as the crows loop and swirl lazily and philosophically overhead.

Not knowing anything about the finer points of unjamming hydraulic quick couplers, Descartes could write, "I think, therefore I am." He was a clever guy, but he wasn't a twenty-first-century man: he was in the middle point of our lives on the earth. If he lived in today's world of shifting angles of perception, he'd have to write, "I am, therefore I am," or "I am, therefore I am bewildered," and then, in keeping with the spirit of his inspiration, "I am bewildered, therefore am I," and after crossing that out, "Am I bewildered? I am. Therefore …" Scratch. Scratch. "Am I bewildered? I am." Scratch. "I am bewildered. Am I?" Damn, hammer the ball-bearing seal of the hose so the pressurized fluid sprays out, then go inside and get a drink.

After living in the silence of the world after beauty, it's damn hard to go home to the imported European image of the earth we call the land. Doris Lessing wrote *African Laughter* after four trips back to her old Southern Rhodesia, once it had gained independence as Zimbabwe and her work to make that independence come about no longer meant exile. It was hard for her. She grew up on a farm in the bush. She watched the eagles and heard the birds sing. Then she had to leave.

In the attitudes and pride and difficulties of the farmers and in so many small cultural details, Lessing's colonial African farm was the same colonial farm I grew up on in the Similkameen. I went to Victoria; she went to London. I returned; she became an accomplished and famous novelist. *Then* she went back. Incredibly, on her first trip she refused to visit her childhood farm at all, feeling that it was the most dangerous thing of all for a writer to discover that the adults of childhood, who carried the glow of gods, were just people: fallible, often broken, ordinary, everyday. Correspondingly, the writer would be, too. The magic would be gone. The source for writing would be gone. We'd all be sitting in a shack in Idaho with Hemingway, thinking about shock treatments and how to tie a good solid knot between a trigger and a piece of string. And you don't want to be thinking too much about that.

Lessing was worrying about nothing. I could have told her that. But then, she found that out for herself when she did eventually drive up onto that hilltop of peach trees and dust, and was a stranger and not a stranger. I learned the same lesson when I went to Toronto with four bottles of homemade wine in my carry-on bag. It was meant to be a thank-you gift to Maria and Heather and a symbol of Thanksgiving. It turned out to be a symbol of power. Doris could have told me. Kim could have told me, if I'd even thought to ask. Anna couldn't have told me, for she lived in the age of beauty, before the beginning of time. Peter tried to tell me. As gently as possible, he tried to tell me that art was dead.

When I finally heard, it was through the medium of a Toronto news producer's cynicism. He had chosen to manipulate a Toronto audience, for his own ends.

"It's about freedom," a woman said. She stood bare-shouldered in a dark, shadowed room. Behind her, dim purple figures danced to electronic music and heavy drums. The camera focussed discreetly on her face: deeply tanned, framed by long black hair. I sat forward on the couch and stared at the small, snowy screen of the TV – Kim's electrons, agitated, glowing. Outside the window it was night. Geese called softly from the reeds. Every evening for the previous two weeks they had been landing in the last light, sinking into the lilac-coloured cloud over the willows. They would leave again at dawn, rising out of powder-blue fog and flying south among the last stars. Winter was coming. "We do here what other people only dream of," the woman said. "We're normal people: accountants, civil servants, professional people. The only thing is: we don't have any hangups. Other people only dream about this." The camera cut to a man hanging four-ounce lead fishing weights to his nipples with clothespins – his face in rapture, intense. Going for the big fish!

I left him to his fishing and wished him luck.

Here in the Cariboo, saffron-robed monks come every summer to perform their rites. On a rock outcropping above an abandoned mineshaft high on a logging road above Cache Creek – sitting on the Trans-Canada Highway and decked out with ten gas stations, one motel set up as a Saharan oasis and another as a castle with bright green battlements, and even a shrine to the Immaculate Conception of Mary – the energies of the universe come together. The monks say you can hear the music of the spheres there, in perfect tones.

Strangely, it was Don Robertson who first told me about the centre of the universe. Retired army major, peacekeeper in Cyprus, editor of the local free newspaper – a collection of ads strung together by a few chunks of text – and long-time freelance fishing writer, he wore a floppy felt hat over his small, sharp eyes, like Humphrey Bogart in *The Maltese Falcon*. I had written of the need to centre Interior BC writing and politics in local culture. That's where Don cut in that he had been researching a fishing story when the owner of the Vidette Gold Mine Resort took him outside and pointed to a grassy slope high above Vidette Lake and explained how Buddhist monks had come, tramped in the hills above the lake, and located the centre of the universe. Don went on to detail a circuitous and vague route through the network of logging roads east of Chasm, to the end of an old mine road. "There was no way I could miss it," he said. He told of how he had sat there, of how in the mountain, the wind in the trees, and the noise of the water, he had sensed that there was no better place in the world.

The idea of a purity of sound in an otherwise clearcut forest enchanted me. It was like going back with Lewis and Clark in 1805 and sighting the Columbia River for the first time, or travelling with Shelley in Switzerland in 1816 and seeing Mont Blanc, a fierce pile of snow and rock, and making of that an image of the mind. This was heady romantic stuff. It was incongruous, too. After all, this is high country, where the strongest form of spirituality you are likely to encounter is a fully loaded logging truck barrelling down at top speed, kicking up a dragon's tail of dust that drifts back for kilometres and settles in a slow fog through the trees. All the trees along the roads are grey. If you walk out through the scrub, you raise clouds of choking dust. Your eyes burn red. You feel dirty.

To the south of the centre of the universe, the Thompson River flows around old ranches, ginseng fields, mobile home parks, a pulp mill, two rail lines, and a massive feedlot stinking up the highway for miles. Fed in troughs right up against the soft shoulder, the cattle stare at the passing traffic while chewing their cud. To the west of the centre of the universe is a vast auto wrecking yard in the sagebrush above the old Hat Creek Ranch – now a provincial heritage site celebrating cowboy culture, formerly the home ranch of Hudson's Bay Company trader and baby killer Donald McLean. From there McLean rode out and terrorized the Shuswap and the Chilcotin with random, brutal violence. Further west still, the region is bounded by the Fraser River, strangely tropical, with the insubstantial, timeless light of a vast river. To the east flows the Thompson, molten snow sweeping green, south out of the Rockies into the desert. Between them all, the plateau itself is a vast, high plain of glacier-scarred basalt overgrown with trees. The Bonaparte River flows lazily through it along a fault line, under high, red, volcanic cliffs.

I first approached the centre of the universe from the north. Ahead of me, the light hung off the edge of the plateau as if there was a big bell of clear glass suspended over the wheatgrass. Stepping off an old ranch trail that started with a rusted, wrecked truck and a collapsing branding corral, I looked down from the edge of the plateau to a black lake snaking below. Believing I was lost, I turned away. Three hours later, I approached it from the south. I met my old tracks at the foot of a grassy knoll.

On top of that knoll, buried between the walls of the canyon and the black water of Vidette Lake, is a small outcropping of bedrock. On it, a fire has been lit, marked now by a few charred lengths of wood soaked by rain and snow.

The wind blows strongly there, rising on one side of the knoll and falling on the other into the valley, through the wind-gnarled branches of an old Douglas fir. Around the crown of the knoll the grass bends to the wind in a circular pattern. In the trees around the knoll, the mosquitoes are intense.

Thirty metres from the centre of the universe lie the ruins of an old cabin; someone lived there once, his front door looking east over the scarred edges of the old lava flows that formed the plateau – ochre, snaking lines meeting the white horizon. So. Some trapper had known where he was. I felt him sitting on his porch in the evening, looking out over the entire world, and farther. I sat with him for awhile.

I returned in early November with my friend Wayne Still, who had learned his Buddhism thirty years earlier planting rice in Taiwan. The last shards of an early snow were dissolving in a black rain. The ground was soaked. The lake below and the mountains to the east and west were lost in scraps of fog. That afternoon, as we ate home-smoked trout, trail mix, and Belle de Boskoop apples, the fog curled around the hill, causing us to appear and disappear. Wayne seemed lost in thought, chewing the edges of his beard. His face sagged. He seemed weary.

"In Buddhism there is no centre to the universe," he said at last. "That's the whole point. So you see why I was interested in seeing this place."

Passing between the droplets of rain, the November wind was biting and cold.

"This place is as good as any other. I guess if you want to bring attention to a particular quality in the universe, and if you want to find a place that represents that quality, you can do that. This is a very ordinary place, but it is remarkably centred."

"I like the way it is contained within a landform," I added, "rather than dominating one."

Sunken between two winding ridges, the hill was a navel, cut in half by the patterns of rainfall. The wet half was treed and dark (although recently logged), the other grassy and golden with light – repeating the larger pattern of the walls of the valley, which were in the same pattern of trees and grass.

Wayne nodded. I had just said the most obvious thing of all.

Wandering in the fog, we discovered a three-hundred-year-old Douglas fir that had been struck by lightning during the previous summer. The lightning had followed the corkscrew grain of the wood to the ground, blasting out a two-inch channel of bark and exposing the yellow wood beneath. The grass around the tree, and the tree's lower bark, were scorched and blackened by fire.

Wayne stroked his beard again. "It's as if someone had said to me, 'I am going to introduce you to God,' and we went there together, stopped in front of a messy, rundown house, walked around back in the weeds, and some guy slid out from underneath an old pickup, with grease on his face, wearing blue overalls, with 'Bob' printed on the pocket and 'Phil's Autobody' stencilled on the back, and my friend said, 'Wayne, I'd like you to meet God. God, I'd like you to meet Wayne.' God reaches a greasy hand forward. We shake hands."

The southern route to the centre of the universe is through the Deadman Valley. The whole one-hour drive north on an ever-narrowing road through ranchland to reserve to old vacation lakes and finally through forests of tall, dark trees, passes along the fault between two geographic plates: on one side, red buttes, jutting headlands, reefs of black rock; on the other, steep cliffs, densely treed. This has obviously been spiritual ground for millennia. It is a wonder the monks spent so long finding it, because it cries out, like a beacon shining from a small airport into the night, a cone of light sweeping among the stars and the green rays of the aurora above black trees. It is no wonder. It is not the centre of the universe that is difficult to find but the path out of one's preconceptions, to see the obvious and to see the centre in the ordinary, the harmed by history, the lost.

I haven't always lived at the centre of the universe. I come from Keremeos, just north of the US border at Nighthawk – one of those border posts where you cruise slowly by the Canada Customs post when heading south because the American agent is most likely there, sharing a coffee or watching a football game on TV. If you drive too fast you have to wait for him to walk the two hundred yards to catch up to you. The road is so hot it shimmers like water. The agent has lots of time. You *will* sweat. When we were heading south last summer we met the agent halfway. He held up a hand to stop us. When I rolled down the window and the heat blew in like a lizard's skin he bent down, looked in, smiled, and said, "Are you lost?"

"No!" For once I could say it like I meant it.

Most of the people near the centre of the universe have moved up from the Coast in the seventies and eighties. When I moved up – in the nineties, not from the Coast but from the Similkameen, and displaced by that same wave of immigration – people were very helpful. They would laugh and say, "You have to understand about small towns. It takes you a few years to get used to it."

"Small town?" I'd say. I'd look around: three grocery stores, two sawmills, an airport, nine restaurants, a mall. Then I'd whisper: "Where?"

On the night the politics of Toronto came to me from the confrontation between the TV production room and the exhibitionist's bar, I turned off the TV in the Cariboo and stepped outside. Shooting stars fell over the black house and the night trees. Raised and trained to be a corporate farmer, yet educated to live in and function in an urban, academic world, I had by that time, through a long process of isolation and discovery, come to see mountains not as shapes of stone and slopes of trees and bunchgrass, but as giants, monsters sleeping around the edges of our clearings: hibernating, watching, living in a slower rhythm. I was living in an ancient, mythic world. By stepping outside that night, I had restored my connection to it. The land is a language. Like all languages you must learn to speak it. I doubted very much if anyone in Toronto would know what I was trying to say, but I thought they would make the attempt. In the spirit of conversation, you understand.

I was wrong. In the brick streets of Toronto, which looked completely European to my British Columbian eyes, people quickly figured out I was from the West. Invariably, when I answered, "Yes, I am from BC," they asked, "How long have you lived in Vancouver?" I'm afraid I didn't react very well.

The writers who asked this question had little time for me, but I had this very conversation with the banker, too, at Thanksgiving. He had time. "Look who's being a snob!" he had answered, grinning. But the charge of snobbism was just a screen – a toastmaster's trick. The real question had to do with who has the authority to speak of the earth: a banker who would contain it within a larger discourse, such as the political structure we have come to call Canada, or a poet and farmer who would contain the "larger" discourse within the earth?

It was a difficult bridge to make. I had just flown in from my high plateau, cut off by two massive rivers and lifted into a realm of hoarfrost and starlight like a lost continent, with a history so secret you can live for twenty years without hearing a word of it. The Ontario poet Al Purdy came to the plateau in the sixties, right about when Anna came to the Similkameen, four hours south. He wrote about horses, Genghis Khan, and cigarettes. Then he left. After Purdy returned to the country of Nortel and investment banking, Coyote, the old Salish trickster, creator, destroyer, and royal fool, slipped out through the sagebrush, owning nothing, giving everything away.

My Canada is built out of fruit trees and black spruce and the Chopaka All-Indian Rodeo. On the few occasions I've ever thought about Toronto, I've thought that Toronto existed to help us build out of these forms a full and independent culture; that by being strong independently we could be strong together. The reality of the last thirty years, and of the unburnable Anna Brown, is that my land is the hinterland and exists to enable Toronto to grow beyond it. Anna wasn't wanted in Toronto; once she left, it carried on as if she had vanished from the world. And she had. When I went to Toronto, I hadn't thought about that yet. I still knew if I brought something local to Canadian literature, I would be given something national, something of equal value, in its place: fair exchange, free trade. I should have asked the cowboys at the Chopaka All-Indian Rodeo. They would have laughed out loud.

At the edge of the neon-blue current along the Thompson River, the icefields build in the still winter water. There, as the stars burn through the lens of the sky, the whistling swans swim between desert mountains covered with snow. On the banks of the river, on old farmland next to the CNR and along the Trans-Canada, people have laid out subdivisions, golf courses, and access roads rimmed with weeds – even a cement plant: the spreading urban/industrial mix. In the midst of that, the swans' earth burns – a power, but one which has absolutely nothing in common with what people have built upon it. It's a strange sight. To live in the subdivisions, and to think that they are part of the land, people have to imagine that they, and their houses, are not there. Weird. The swans cling to the earth because it is all that they have. It is all any of us have.

Wayne was responsible for the earth I brought to Toronto. When I met him, he had just returned to Canada after a decade travelling in India, Nepal, Japan, Australia, Bali, and Taiwan. His hair was long. He wore a loose shirt of Indonesian cotton that fell almost to his knees, and heavy wool pants from Peru. A long, heavy belt cord hung down from his side. He wore heavy leather boots, scuffed at the toes: GWG Kodiaks. The steel safety shell glinted through the leather. His cabin had a screen door, a giant stag-horn sumac bush, and two rooms.

"I built this last winter," he said behind me as I stepped in. The cabin consisted of a bunk and a combined kitchen and dining room. Through the open door, the robins were calling for rain. The living room was outside: a bench under the sumac, facing south over the US border at Nighthawk to Chopaka, the blue mountain at the foot of the valley – traditionally a woman, her back swirling in the green eddies of the lower river, an erect nipple standing out against a blue sky, her eyes closed, tenderly.

"I couldn't travel my whole life," Wayne said, after he'd made licorice tea and we sat at the oilcloth-draped table. "I wasn't going back to Toronto, and I wasn't going back to the Prairies, so I came here. The farms are small." A grey-pink stream of incense curled up beside his head. The incense stick was jammed in sand in a cracked coffee cup. The thick smoke curled up and swam and sang along the ceiling. A few stray wisps swirled lower, around our faces.

"I grew up on a farm in Saskatchewan. Life was very strict. My father was a Calvinist. Everything had to be in its place. I was not in my place. I was whipped. When I was eighteen, I ran away to Toronto. It was too big a shock. I discovered that there was a world. That was when I decided to go travelling.

I spent six months doing nothing but sitting in an apartment, watching TV. I tried marriage, too. Everything was a prison. I had to get away. In Buddhism we don't believe in the reality of this world.

"On the farm in Saskatchewan, I drove the tractor every day. The skies went on forever. That was farming. Our house was sheltered in a yard of thorn trees to keep out the cold winds. I went back there. The farm had been sold. It's part of a larger farm now. The house had been abandoned. The newspapers that we insulated it with were still on the walls. My father's belt that he whipped us with was still hanging on the back of the door. It was depressing. But it was home. The land that raises you stays a part of your karma. It's woven through you. It's one of the places you centre yourself in."

Wayne wasn't the only one who had gone to the East in those years for wisdom. The Vancouver experimental writer Dave Cull, the Tish poet, "the guy who ran the mimeograph machine," as he put it, vanished for a decade and a half: poof! – like a kidney bean under a water glass. Maybe he was thinking of Rimbaud going to the Sudan, running guns – the poet's temptation to act, like Coleridge thinking he was going to pack up the Susquehanna and grow cotton: poetry accepted, and *lived*. Dave, however, did it one better than Coleridge: he built a Buddhist temple in New Zealand – on his own. It was no small feat. One day, however, Dave realized that he was being had: he was serving New York businessmen who would come out for a few weeks' spiritual holiday a year, while he was just getting older. He came home. He lives in Parksville on Vancouver Island, retirement country for Anna's compatriots who stayed and only late in life are making the same move away from the world to the eternal and romantic land – but this time with the security of front-loaded mutual funds, and without the complications of children. Dave fixes up run-down houses and rents them cheap to young single mothers on welfare. Sometimes he brings out his signed, hand-bound copy of Olson late at night and sets it in the middle of a bare table in a low light.

F reshly back from university in Victoria to make my peace with the land I had learned to hate only a few years before – seeing it as a prison that kept me from the city – in Wayne's presence I began to lose a sense of the valley as a collection of farms and to gain a new one of a wild earth, scarcely touchable, but strong, and smelling of dust. In that earth, the silver wind of the river poured like a slow fire over stones that seemed so thin in the midday heat they were only a thin sheen of light on an infinite and trembling darkness.

Our employer, Brian Mennell, had bought a vineyard that year, hoping to leave the orchards behind, to move forward into a form of agriculture with guaranteed markets. I pounded posts. It was brutal. Every night for six weeks I would come back to the cabin, my senses deadened. Wayne would be there, a stack of hives in the back of his old yellow '67 Chev pickup – "Old Yeller," he called her. He would be nailing new frames together from freshly cut pine he had stacked beside him under the sumac. His hammering was soft. It smelled of shavings. He would have spent the day blossom-thinning peaches in the orchard behind the cabin, with the pink petals shaking down off the limbs. When I came up the path from the dry bed of Cawston Creek, he would put down his hammer. We would talk about the Tao, about Buddha.

"Be careful of knowledge and education," he would say. "It is difficult to learn anything at a university. I hope you are going to become the poet of the revolution."

He would grin – his bad teeth showing through his long beard.

Wayne worked his bees in partnership with Brian. At four in the morning, when the stars still lay over the valley like flecks of foam above the deep pools of the river, he would start up Old Yeller. Her headlights would beam through the night, into the cabin where I lay in my sweat, sweep along the walls, and she would rattle off down the gravel and shale driveway to the Indian Reserve, south, with Wayne's big grey Norwegian elkhound perched on the toolbox in the back, gulping down the wind.

Living with Wayne that summer was like living with the California Beat poet Gary Snyder – Wayne could as easily tear down the transmission of his pickup on the gravel and thistles and wireweed in front of the cabin as discuss the illusory appearances of this world and the hidden structures that lie behind it.

"If you believe in nothing," I asked, "and in the nothingness of this world, what is this world around us? How is that a prescription for life?"

"You must understand," he said. "Writing a poem or painting a picture is no more or less creative than a carpenter planing a board or building a house. Everything we do is either creative or destructive. All creative acts should be honoured. If what we do is not creative, it will destroy us. The world is an illusion, but it is also a tool. The world is something we can use to be born again as another spirit."

Late at night the crickets sang to the wind their songs of the ancient civilizations of the grasses. The night wrapped itself around the cabins, electric and alive. I would sit at Wayne's table, in the insect-thick air. A hand-rolled beeswax candle, shaped from the wax foundation of a frame, would burn before us: a small genie dancing a foot off the oilcloth. Wayne would open his copy of the Tao and would speak of the Nothing that has generated the world, of his time among the dervishes in Turkey, the way the dust kicked up around their feet, achieving absolute stillness through motion, spinning the mind free from the body.

"Jesus was a dervish," he said one night. The stars broke in a high surf over the roof.

A s I was killing hornets one day in late August, Wayne and Brian's brother Robert appeared suddenly on the driveway, wearing white bee suits, with veils over their faces.

"You seen a swarm of bees?" called Robert, stomping past, a small tin pot smoking with grass in his hand.

"No bees! But there are a lot of hornets!" The hornets had little nests among the apples. The day before I had mistaken one for an apple and had leapt off the top of the ladder yelling. I had hit the ground running. Now I was doing something about it.

Wayne came up behind Robert, carrying a section of a hive called a super, taking long strides, with his wedding veil over his face.

"Having fun?" he asked.

I stood there for a moment, dappled with light and shade, like a deer among the trees.

The swarm hung off the end of a branch like a small image of the sun, golden, humming loudly: a model of a large and complex atom, the electrons spraying out. Wayne and Robert moved slowly, silently, white-suited. The bees darted out, fat and sluggish, gorged on honey. With the black shadow of bees flashing over him on their elliptical orbits, Wayne held his super under the bees as Robert picked up a fencepost and smashed the branch hard. With hardly a tremor, the bees fell from the branch into the box. As they fell, they exploded into a wide mass, like a slow-motion wave. Wayne set the super down quickly, and Robert slammed a lid on it and jammed the smoker into the entrance hole. All the bees that had not fallen in flashed around them angrily, settling on their hats and veils and white, cotton-gloved hands. As Wayne and Robert moved away, the bees left them one by one and swarmed angrily around the poplar branch, looking for their queen – but she was not there.

The next summer, Wayne bought a farm. In a clearing where he had pushed out half a dozen McIntosh trees, he built a house. Actually, he built a basement: it sat there, the pitched, peaked silver roof of old printing plates rising out of his garden of garlic and cabbages.

The roof was intriguing: Campbell's Soup is on special at Super-Valu: upside down and backwards. "Lost, one Golden Retriever, answers to the name Chubby … "

"I'll show you the house," Wayne said, giving me the grand tour. "This is my workshop." He was talking about fully half of the basement. The air was full of the ginger, nutmeg, and sagebrush scent of honey. A few bees sat, pulsing, on his tools. Running across the back of the basement was the honey room: tile-floored, cold, with a gleaming stainless steel centrifuge, and hives stacked from floor to ceiling.

The living quarters were off to the side: two hundred square feet, with a stove, a counter, a sink, a small table, a woodstove, bookshelves, and a bed. The walls were done in rough, unplaned one-by-six fir, with long strands of wood curling off them, and knotholes, and crystals of pitch oozing out of the grain of the wood.

"I'll live down here for three years," he said.

It is twenty years later as I write this. Wayne has never moved upstairs. He never will. Everything he owns smells of honey now. Every book on his shelf is coated with an eighth of an inch of pollen.

In that second summer, Brian's vineyard was dead from winter frost. That July, thunderheads grew every day along the ridgelines as Wayne and I swung our hoes among the dead vine stumps. The clouds towered, immense and high along the north wall of the valley, above the Okanagan, evaporating off the lakes with the heat.

"The Himalayas are like that," Wayne said one day, leaning against his hoe, a quarter of a tempered disc-harrow blade bolted to a six-foot handle two inches thick at its base. "You walk there in the valleys at twelve thousand feet. The mountains rise above you on the far side, above the green meadows and the step-roofed temples. You look up, then you tilt your head and look up further. You can't take it in – they are too immense. It is a sacred experience. We are so small." Then he lifted his hoe again and started chopping.

In the late afternoon, skeins of hail would drift down over the high slopes. The air would shake with distant thunder. In the dark, a fast wind would sweep up against the cabin, then the rain would be there, cold in the night, gentle, sifting down. As the dawn sun burned like a meadow of red clover over the Indian reserve at the bottom of the valley, the world would smell clear. A few clouds would hang against the side of the mountain, caught and tangled in the trees. By seven, they would have all burned away. The sky would be as blue as the wild forget-me-nots in the speargrass.

Once, just before dawn, a yellow ball of light slowly and soundlessly floated down. The whole storm went silent and still. The ball drifted directly into the six-inch-square top of a cedar vineyard post and disappeared. Rapidly, the rain became a thin drizzle, catching and tearing on the wind, and the lightning moved off into the larches and the peat lakes of the high country. It was too muddy for work. I walked over to Wayne's. He listened. He ran his fingers through his beard. "Everything is alive," he said.

"What I don't understand," I said, "is how if you believe in nothing and in the vanity of all human perceptions, you can own a farm and have a mortgage and work? That doesn't make sense to me."

"Everything in the world has a spirit. Even the transmission of my truck. I can work with that spirit. I can take the Buddha apart and put him back together again!" He laughed. "You have to understand: Buddhism is not about renouncing the world, but about entering it completely and working within it. Everything has its opposite: you take that opposite away and nothing exists. The world is illusion. The yogis are able to control their breath until that breath is conscious: they are that breath. It connects them with the world.

It is an illusion, but without that illusion of a world there is no world. You can achieve Zazen through spirit. There are lots of ways of working with spirit. No one way is better than any other."

I got a bear in my hives," said Wayne another day. I stood on the other side of the grape row, my bush scythe upended on its handle, scraping my stone along the blade.

"Yeah?" I felt the blade with my thumb. "Did he get everything?"

"No, but he made a big mess. He destroyed two hives and knocked over two more. They were full of honey – two hundred pounds each. The bees were pretty mad this morning."

"What are you going to do? Shoot him?"

"I can't *shoot* him. He has a soul too. Someday I might be reincarnated as a bear. They are powerful, beautiful animals. They've been worshipped for ten thousand years. I just don't want them to mess with my hives, the bastards!"

I ran the stone along the scythe again. A fine carborundum dust flaked off the stone as it screeched over the blade.

"Any bear that comes back is going to have a surprise," he said.

A meadowlark stood on a post behind him and called out loudly across the air. Wayne smiled. A second meadowlark echoed back faintly from a tree on the edge of his orchard next door.

"You going to wait for him all night?" I asked. I ran my thumb over the blade again and passed the stone over.

"Are you kidding?" He laughed and quickly ran the stone from the tip of his blade back to the handle. "Better yet. I'm going back this afternoon. I'll surround the hives with a wire fence. Barbed wire." He spoke between the strokes of his stone. "I'm going to hang a dozen cans of sardines off the wire." Stroke. "Just opened a little bit, so the oil drips out and he can smell the fish." Stroke. "I'm going to cut those cans open as jagged and rough as I can." Stroke. "And I'm going to hook the whole thing up to a fencer and run 25,000 volts through it!" Stroke. "You've got to think like a bear! He'll come alright. He won't be able to resist it." Stroke. "But he'll have one hell of a surprise!" He handed the stone back to me across the wire. "It'll be like fucking World War I."

"How are you going to power the fencer?"

"Solar power." He laughed again. "It'll be like fucking Vietnam."

We started to scythe again down the row, matching each other swathe by swathe. Ahead of us the red root pigweed and lambsquarter stood six feet tall. Behind us they were chopped low and clean.

At ten o'clock one Sunday morning, in a sun already so bright it was almost blinding, we sat around our table under the open roof of the workers' kitchen, nursing our heads from the party the night before. Among the half-full beer bottles on the counter, Luc was heating water to boil for coffee, the old kettle groaning through the quarter-inch-thick scale of calcium on its element. We settled down to wait. It usually took about twenty-five minutes to heat four cups of water. Luc turned on his tape deck: Manitas de Plata.

"He's a gypsy," said Luc. "They travel around. Every summer they have a huge gathering in a forest in southern France. They play music and dance. This guy's the best of all. He doesn't even have a name anymore, just Hands of Silver – *manitas de plata*." As the kettle groaned and creaked and ticked, and Manitas de Plata strummed and beat on the side of his guitar, François pulled his own guitar out from beside the fridge, and sitting there with a cigarette hanging loosely out of his lips, softly began to play along – not to any tune, but just picking out single strings here and there, lifting up short melodies and letting them fall, slower than the music.

When the coffee was ready, Luc strained it into a wide-mouth canning jar. An ant ran around the rim. Luc passed me some halvah on the tip of his knife: breakfast. He had just lived for a year on a kibbutz. I tasted it: it was sweet, and crumbled like ash on my tongue. Denis – who would soon quit to return to Quebec and sell life insurance – was hanging out his wash on strings he'd tied between the two-by-four pillars of the roof, and draping it over the sagebrush on the bank that tumbled down beside us.

"Hey!" he called – the only English he knew. I went over. Luc came with a cup of coffee and handed it to Denis. With Denis's laundry in a bucket beside us on the concrete, we watched as ants fought over territory on the cactus and speargrass slope. The battle was between tiny black fire ants and big black-and-red weaver ants four times their size. They marched on each other in long columns, forming huge pincer movements and encirclements – a tangled mass of red and black bodies by the thousands, shifting like a carpet weaving and unweaving itself. From one side, twenty-foot-long columns of fire ants poured out of holes in the sand and marched in. From the other side, a long column of weaver ants came out of the sagebrush on the hill above us. In the end, the fire ants won the battle. They attacked the weaver ants ten at a time, threw them on their backs, and chewed off their legs. From both sides, ants carried their dead from the battlefield. After half an hour there were no weaver ants left, only the fire ants, relentlessly prowling the ground.

Manitas de Plata had long since stopped playing. Our coffee was cold. We were all silent.

As the morning light came in through the white, sprinkler-stained glass of my cabin window that second summer, the sun built up golden inside the room. Every minute it glowed brighter and brighter, like the breath of a bee. Outside, the vines were still churning from the night wind. The wind was pooling in the wireweed, in tiny rivers and back eddies of dust. There was a form to all of it. It was that form, that stillness, that immediate perception, which Wayne tried to teach me with the Tao. He showed me his tools plainly, the practical work of the Buddhist: tear down a transmission, build a beehive, bake a loaf of bread. I never managed to get more than broken moments into my poetry, however, yet outside of poetry I lived the air that summer, more and more every day. My hands gloved with light as I worked. The mountains rose above me, shimmering. A red-tailed hawk screamed overhead. Literature, which had brought me to this awareness of the living earth, was being sloughed off, replaced by the world, cell by cell and molecule by molecule and waving tree branch by waving tree branch, until suddenly it wasn't there any longer. Now, after twenty years of living in that new earth, the world of words seems to me puzzling and strange, as the substance of the earth was before, yet I use words, for they too have spirit.

The year I met Wayne was the year Anna died. The world was ceasing to make sense. That was the year my parents left their own conversation with the land and bought a new, even more industrial farm down south, across the line. When I pulled into their cherry orchard at Benton City, my brother, Roland, was out riding with Jim, the alcoholic Vietnam vet, son of my parents' partner, the biggest fruit grower in the state. They rode three-wheeled motorcycles in the Horse Heaven Hills, shooting rattlesnakes to chop up into steaks, cutting off their heads and throwing them into burlap sacks bungee-corded to their carrier racks. When Jim and Roland brought the snakes back in the 105-degree heat, they were half-cooked and rotten and smelled real bad. Jim threw them all away in the greasewood and sagebrush on the far side of the concrete ditch that brought the water from the Columbia to the southern side of the orchard – BC water, signed away. The soil of the orchard was pure sand. The water just sank straight through. But it was Jim I was really interested in – he had a greasy Bardall cap turned backwards on his head, his beard was scruffy and untrimmed, his hair was tangled, greasy, blonde. His voice was surprisingly loud.

My father: "He had such promise. He could have taken over the orchard, the best damn cherry orchard in the world, but then he went to Vietnam; when he came back he was a mess and could never get himself straightened out. He got into drugs. His father wouldn't even hire him anymore. He couldn't trust him. He wasn't reliable. You couldn't give him an important job. Drugs will do that. Shit."

Doris Lessing should have been there. In all the years of my childhood there had been no difference between this desert and the one we lived in at home, yet at that moment I could see, in Jim, all at once, that it was not home at all. It was like reading a tourist brochure on Whidbey Island on the Washington Coast – THE WHIDBEY ISLAND NAVAL AIR SQUADRON, "THE SOUND OF FREEDOM," declaim the billboards – as the fighters roar low overhead, above the nuclear submarine base. The brochure talks glowingly of a quaint Mark Twain guesthouse in the country.

There are two worlds. One is the world of objects. The other is the world of perceptions. In the world of objects, where words are used to manipulate truth, orchards are not called orchards, but ranches: *fruit ranches*. They are a thousand acres apiece: impossibly large. There in the Yakima Valley there is no possibility of "land", or "relationship to land". You can't even talk about it. What you do is call up the Uniroyal pesticide agent on your car phone. You read the temperature off electric dials as you cruise slowly through the blocks, phone up the foreman, and tell him to turn on the overhead sprinklers to keep off the frost. You keep your cherry trees at a point of drought just short of collapse, so the cherries, soft and dehydrated, can soak up the rain and have enough capacity in their cells not to split, order the Mexicans to pick them, shove them through a bath of ice water, and hire fifty women from town wearing shorts and halter tops to pack them, suddenly big, juicy, firm – and flavourless. You ship them east on Amtrak, forty carloads a night. I had been offered that power.

"Look at this town," said my father, as he drove us through the green, locust-lined streets of Benton City in the hot and dusty air. "There's nothing here, yet the young people all stay. They don't have any grand ideas. They just want to drive out in their cars on Saturday nights and fuck and have babies. That's the only fun they know. Isn't it great?"

I turned the opportunity down. After a few short months with Wayne, I had become something my parents in all their years of immigrant assimilation had not achieved: I had *become* a stranger. They had started off that way and had only become Canadians – and were then attempting to become Americans – by renouncing their strangeness. In contrast, as the second and third generation on this shoulder of the earth,

I only became a Canadian by moving back into that space they had abandoned and re-imagining it. I looked out over the Yakima Valley, not to see the farms there, but to see the landscape as it would have been without them, and to live in that, with the volcanoes running in a white line along the Pacific shore to the west, the green mountains in between, and the meandering, willow-throated, snake-green river below.

At first, the septic tank of my cabin was just a ten-foot-deep hole in the gravel. The hole stayed there for weeks, empty. One day, Brian unfolded a sheet of paper on the spray-stained green hood of his tractor – the diagram of a steer, with every cut of meat highlighted and named: brisket, chuck, flank steak, rump roast, eye of round. Butcher by numbers.

The steer was in the pen in the lowland at the base of the cottonwoods, black and scraggly-haired, his rump smeared perpetually with manure, his eyes small, with one crooked horn and a bad attitude. Whenever anyone came by, he charged the fence. It made you jump.

Wayne, the vegetarian, studied the paper and smiled. "Just cut along the dotted line, right, Brian?" He reached for Brian's knife and ran his thumb across the blade. "Mmmmm! Nice and sharp!"

We stood there for a minute, watching Brian round the corner of the shed past the lilacs. The chickens scattered up in the cabbages as he kicked past, two knives in one hand, a rifle in the other, a map in his back pocket. The last we saw was his red hair glowing, then it dipped around the corner.

"It'll be a slaughter," said Wayne.

The bones and guts and hide of the cow wound up in the pit behind my cabin. Brian's jeans were dark with blood, he had bandages on two of his fingers, and he had no shirt. He lifted the bucket of the tractor and dumped the guts of the steer into the hole with a splash. "I'll come back and cover it in tomorrow!" he yelled. As he drove away, the sagebrush glowed, a faint, pale orange in the low angles of the late sun, as the sun rose up into the brilliant, neon-yellow flowerheads. They looked like Hopi kachinas, watching me from the bunchgrass. The roar of the tractor sounded fainter and fainter. The sunlight fell out of the clouds. In the dark I walked to the cabin. The air was grey, like a thousand moths dancing. I read Rudolf Steiner that night, of his hierarchies of angels, of bending the laws of matter by the action of the mind, while behind me the flies festered and the guts swelled. In the morning I definitely knew something was not right. My fears were supported by Wayne.

"The karma's not right," he said. "I wouldn't stay there until he fills that thing in."

"Well, it'll certainly get the septic system going!"

"It's bad karma. You better hope he gets it covered in soon."

It wasn't funny. After a week and a half, only my absolute fatigue let me sleep even a little in the stink. The worst was the flies. They hatched out of that meat and flooded the cabin by the thousands. They covered the outside of the windows. If I went out there, big swarms of heavy, swollen, black flies, shimmering green on their thoraxes, would settle on me and crawl. Every time I asked Brian about it, he would smile disarmingly and say, "Tomorrow."

About that time the police stopped Brian on the back road into town, along the mountain. When they got a good look at his Volkswagen, they told him that if they ever caught him driving that thing again, they'd throw him in jail. So one day we towed the Volkswagen over to the vineyard and tipped it into the pit. I fit the PVC pipe of the drain together, ran it in through the driver's window, and Brian began to dump the gravel. The last we saw of that overturned car was its four bald tires sticking up from its belly. Then I walked across the levelled pit and jumped up and down on the gravel a couple of times for good measure. Wayne passed me a drink of garlic. We drank. When the bottle was empty, he filled it with water and walked to the middle of the pit and poured it on the sand and rocks. Then we left. I had my scythe over my shoulder and a sharpening stone in my back pocket. Wayne had his twenty-pound brush hoe.

"Those flies are really something!" he roared.

"You can say that again," I said, not quite so enthusiastically.

"Isn't life amazing!"

The sun was over us like a clove of garlic, sweating a heavy oil.

That's what it's like to go back. That's what Lessing might have found: myth surviving in our own age, people larger than life and brokenly human at the same time. That's what Coleridge might have found with Southey in the pantisocratic community they planned for Maryland in 1794. Instead of following through with his plan to go back to the land and homestead there, he chickened out. We got dreams of paradise, on the edge of consciousness, scarcely remembered. We got the modern world: romantic dream journey, opium haze, hero quest.

We got an albatross hanging around the neck.

With this deep, intimate, and often troubled history of the land behind me, I flew into the dream world, the magma core of our time, like a sweating hero in a story by Edgar Rice Burroughs, hacking aside vines with a machete. What I found out is that Toronto has a new language of its own and Toronto goes on forever. You can fly into Toronto and you can fly out, but there is no way to drive out of Toronto. It can't be done: the earth is no longer real there. As you drive through Toronto, buildings rise up and fall back, rhythmically. It's like trying to read an ancient script cut deep into clay tablets: you can see the pattern, and you can feel it makes sense, in the way music makes sense, yet like music there are no words. Worse yet, unlike reading any other language, of Toronto you can never be sure: maybe it is the buildings that remain still and the land is like a treadmill, spilling out behind. It's disorienting: obviously, either the city does not exist, or the world does not exist – you can't have them both at the same time, and you can't be without at least one of them at all times. A classic paradox! As I drove down the floating night-time streets of Toronto, I felt like a German physicist in the thirties, poring over blurry black-and-white photographs of subatomic particles that were both waves and particles and were neither, while all around him the world was falling into war, and Heidegger was toying with fascism and inventing a philosophy of existence for our time, powered by the nuclear conversion of matter into ethics: splitting atoms; splitting hairs.

Toronto, like Paris or Berlin, is a city of dreams. Like other dreams and other cities it is terrible and compelling and exciting all at the same time, and stands just at the edge of reason, like a statue of Mary, painted blue and gold, at a crossroads outside of St. Mihel, and the fog pooling on the narrow road, with no road signs: they were blown off in a war a while back and it was felt prudent to leave them off. Who knows where dreams lead. Find your own way.

2

HOMEMADE

WINE

I flew into the city of dreams in the dark. There was only a handful of stars, pale as the illustrations in a book of sky charts for children. My daughter has a book like that, with a cardboard star-wheel pinned to the back cover. As she spins the pale blue sky and aluminum stars of the wheel, Ursa Major drinks the horizon and the seasons rise and fall like waves, in bioluminescent foam. I recognized the book immediately, but either it had grown very large or I had become very small. I was over a field of light. It was like lifting the cover off my old Apple IIE computer – a monthly ritual, to press down the chips – with the green-and-gold circuitboards lying there, warm under my fingers. Maria wore a hand-knit, natural white wool sweater. She stood tiredly a little to the side of the luggage carousel.

"Harold?" she asked.

"Maria?" It was like a dubbed black-and-white movie.

We didn't know what to talk about. For a minute we stood in awkward silence, watching the suitcases go round and round on the carousel. Then Maria said, "You look just like the picture on your book."

My arm ached. Stuffed with four tall brown and green bottles of wine – Gewürztraminer and Cabernet Sauvignon from a vineyard on the glacial cliffs above Skaha Lake – my carry-on bag weighed a ton. Late the December before, half singing to each other in the afternoon after a day racking the heavy twelve-gallon carboys, my friend Gord and I had carried that wine out into the snow so the cold would bring the acid out against the swollen walls of the glass. Venus was burning through the pale sky – the colour of a robin's egg – as we set the jugs down. It was the hour of a winter afternoon when there are no shadows, and all things – trees, houses, grass, and even the air – are on fire with themselves: the light has bound completely with them, and instead of reflecting off their surfaces, shines from within them. I had been so happy with our work that I had taken a picture of the wine. When Maria and her partner Heather asked for ideas for a cover to my book, I sent them a big envelope stuffed with sketches of iodine blotches, houseflies, screen doors, outlines of bandages slapped across the cover: visual puns on the satiric content of the poems. Just as I was about to close the envelope, I slipped in my photo of one hundred and eighty gallons of wine sitting out in the snow. The wine shone: soft blues and yellows and greens in those carboys and water jugs and one old hand-blown muriatic acid vat, stamped 1922. They used it.

W ine-making is an ephemeral art, as rigorous as calculus, and despite recent attempts to codify the range of human taste on a cardboard wine-wheel – "hints of raspberry and blackcurrant" on the one side to "traces of skunk and kerosene" on the other – wine can't really be codified or touched. It is not a form of objectivity or distance, but rather of surrender: it leads away from words and what has been contained in them. You take a drink of wine and you step into the flow of time, which is like a fish jumping in a still, black, evening lake: the ripples spread outwards, slowly, dark, green-shouldered, stilling until they disappear and once again only the lake is there – only to be broken somewhere else, then somewhere else again. That is history. The wine will take you there. The first juice pours out of the press into white, plastic, honey buckets. A wine glass is held briefly under the dark stream. There is the sudden taste of the earth again, the old wine staring out at us, cool, through the veil of the sugars. It is electrifying.

One day I opened my door into the wind on the Middle Bench Road in Keremeos. A small, thin man in tall rubber boots stood there, smiling. He wore a blue beret cocked on his head.

"Hi, my name is Joe," he said, in a thick French accent. "I have heard about you. We men of the land must stick together." He held out to me two half-gallon bottles of wine: one was brown-yellow; the other a deep red, like the gills of fish. He smiled, toothless.

I got out two glasses and we tried it.

It tasted of a day in late October, as the sun comes through the clouds, and the sky is blue and thin, and the ground is frozen six inches deep, and the grape leaves hang dead and a deep, muddy brown off the vines. The sparrows rise out of the pigweeds like a shout swallowed inside the air and hang there, briefly, and settle down, like fish on a riverbed of gravel and sand, like a whale, breathing, then diving again.

I was lost.

Ten years after Anna died, after I met Wayne, after I learned that the earth is more vital than the images we make of the earth, after I discovered that words can just as well be used to lead away from words to the earth – where no words can follow – as they can be used to lead away from the earth to a concrete-and-glass world where the earth is a rumour of long ago, I was making wine with Gord in that old muriatic acid jar from UBC, still in its original wooden packing case. There were big bubbles in the deep, olive-green glass. When it was cold, and snow lay over the grass behind the house – in the dark days of the year when there was never any sun – we set up an old Arborite table by the leafless kiwi vine. As dusk settled over the house and yellow light streamed up the stairwell into the coarse old snow, we carried up the heavy jugs one at a time and set them on the table. Nights, after Christmas, with the tungsten stars above us, when a black, volcanic glass had replaced the air, to stand out there in the Similkameen wind was to be breathless. We would hurry inside and shut the door. The old, leaded windows were sheets of black slate. While we were inside, the carboys would sit all night, at eight degrees below freezing, and be as clear as the air. The stars would pool in them, grey and dark. In that cold, the acid would crystallize, and in a slow breath, days in the shadowless light, nights in the total blackness of the wind, the wine would grow still over a week, like parsnips left out in the garden that only grow sweet after the first frost. Then we would bring the carboys inside again and let them rest – like divers depressurizing after a dive into the deep ocean.

Our grapes came from Bill Holt's vineyard at Chopaka. The vineyard doesn't look like much, lying along the river on a fan of alluvial shale and orange dust: one hundred and twenty acres of vineyard fifteen years ago. Big blocks of land stood empty even then. Now only thirty-five acres are planted. The rest is gone to high, wild yellow grass, a few posts, a few wires. Even in midsummer the grass is yellow. Piles of posts are scattered around the rutted-out driveways. There's a five-acre orchard down by the river, cut down and left as stumps; a greenhouse for raising young grape plants, the plastic torn; fallen piles of bins and wires, and scattered throughout it a few small blocks – sometimes one acre, sometimes ten – of grapes, in no set pattern, tilled clean, with the plants rising straight off the stalks, feathering the air, and the sun soaking through them. On that derelict, post-industrial farm, Bill grew the best grapes in the country. Below the vineyard and the dead waste fields, the cottonwoods tower out of the marshy bottomland. The water cuts silver-blue along the feet of the mountain on the far western valley wall and then swings across the floodplain until it curls away again in rapids at the lower corner of the vineyard, then under the Chopaka Indian Reserve Bridge. All summer long, young mosquitos flood in huge clouds through the air, in a wall towering fifty metres above the current. They hang there, suspended, caught in the light like drops of rain.

In the loading yard, four bins of grapes would be waiting for us, in the weeds and the piles of splintered shale. One tractor, bleeding oil and grease, would be hulking down, a giant lizard, heavy, brooding, unblinking. We'd sit in our trucks for a minute while the dust rolled over us like a pack of wild dogs. Then we'd swing out. Despite the late fall days, it would be hot. Grasshoppers, already frozen ten miles north in Keremeos, would rise from the weeds, clacking furiously, coasting in front of us, or would smash into our chests and tumble to the ground. They'd splay their red wings wide and sail. A cloud of starlings would seep in from the cottonwoods, their shadows swooping by underfoot on the soil, dark, so that with starlings above us and below us we'd be within the flock, turning and wheeling quickly over the land. They'd settle suddenly into the grapes two hundred and fifty metres up the slope and disappear among the leaves, chirping wildly, a bright sound filling the whole air.

Suddenly Bill would be there, walking uphill out of the high weeds, smiling: a thin, tall, craggy man with dark black hair, never combed, and a few days of black stubble. He'd be wearing big rubber boots, torn jeans, and a checked shirt, the sleeves tightly rolled up. A pack of cigarettes would be tucked in above his left elbow. His mouth would slip into a sideways grin as he would come up to us and calmly shake a cigarette out of the box and light it. He'd spend the rest of our time there puffing on it, biting it in and out of his mouth or leaving it dangling.

"The birds are eating everything," he'd say.

The lizard tractor would roar, and its big tires would hunker down deep into the dust. Blue smoke and the crude-oil stink of 90W transmission lube would flood over us. It smelled of dinosaurs, fern-trees, and ancient marshes. Bill would sit on the torn yellow seat, brush the hydraulic controls lightly with his fingers, settle the bins in place, back the tractor up, and leave it idling, so we'd have to shout – small figures in a heat haze: bang! bang! bang! bang! bang! As we'd leave, the grasshoppers would flash up out of the high grass. A hawk would sit on a vineyard pole, a vole in its talons, and turn its head to follow us as we drove past. He'd fall into his wings and flap slowly across the grass to the river. The shade of clouds would skitter over the valley floor and bend at right angles and continue up the cliffs, moving, like ships across the land.

The wine we made was Gewürztraminer. The Gewürztraminers of Alsace are heavy in the glass, like the heavy light of Europe that hangs in the air: something you can cut with a knife. Standing in Baden, or Voegtlinshoffen, or on the Kaiserstuhl, and looking over the vineyards and the church spires is like looking into the physical manifestation of time itself. It's not in the land. It's in the air. As much as the land is the physical record of time there, so is the grey and towering sky: a dense, crystalline pattern, like the human brain. It is all the time that has ever passed in the world and all the time that will pass but has not yet revealed itself, like a fresco, faded and pale on a church wall, flaking off. It tastes like gold.

The Gewürztraminers of the Okanagan are bright and clear, pale straw in colour, with little devils of light skipping around in the glass and stars of light spraying through the cupped wine, like a breath blown into a ball and hanging there before you for a moment on the air – held in the hand but not touched by the hand. In a good year such as 1992 they have the mulled-wine spices so characteristic of this variety, splashing over the tongue and still tingling there after the wine is swallowed, like grape leaves fluttering back to stillness after a sudden gust of wind kicks up in the dust and splashes through them, giving them for a moment the energy of birds. It tastes of the sun, blowing in yellow and white squalls against the purple hills, and the lake so far below, a totally different colour from the sky, glowing. It gives you back the unsteadiness in the legs, with sky both above and below you, and the steel skies of winter, and the glacial stone that holds that colour throughout the summer. It has all that. But it does not have the European full-bodied, deep wooden cello cry and depth of time. The Gewürztraminers of the

Okanagan are youthful wines – the play of the sun over leaves and over the lake, blowing down out of the pine forests. Though the earth can be tasted in them, it is not a heavy soil. It is thin, glacial soil, tasting of alkaline salts and wild grasses and shepherd's purse, with hardly any organic matter at all.

"You have to remember," says Harry McWaters of Sumac Ridge Wines in Summerland, "that the vines in Alsace are a hundred years old. You can get heavy wines from old wood. Our vines are all very young. The oldest of them are only ten years old, but we can notice a difference even in those: they get stronger, spicier."

Just as I was to do later in Toronto, I once brought a bottle of Gewürztraminer that Gord and I had made in his basement kitchen to the Ruhr. I poured it into the heavy German crystal – each glass had a cut-glass ball halfway up the stem. In each ball was a small reflection of the pool of wine in the glass, a yellow ripple of light, swaying, pinched between the fingers. The words came fast: "This is better than anything we can get in Alsace!" I agreed: the wines of Alsace have an unequalled richness, but they are cool wines, smelling of old stone and wild boars in the woods, and acorns, and grey air, while our wine was all splash and light, uncontainable by the glass, filling the room, laughing.

Gord rummages around in the drawers of his Elvis-era kitchen, with the red plastic knobs on the cupboards and the checkered linoleum, and out of the clang and crash of glass and metal sliding around each other like an orchestra tuning up, he pulls out a strange object and holds it up proudly.

"Ha!" he laughs. "A horse syringe." And it's big, too: six inches long. It can hold a half cup of serum. Gord slips an eight-inch length of siphon hose on the end of it. I lift an airlock from the muriatic acid bottle. The bubble falls out of the lock like mercury. Gord dips the end of the syringe into the wine and slowly draws the plunger back. As the chamber fills with a rich, golden liquid, the fruit esters flood the room. With the gold bee light and honey caught in the syringe he lifts it carefully. I set the airlock back in as Gord pushes the plunger down to slowly fill two glasses. The wine is heavy and full. "We've done it!" laughs Gord. "It was a funny year last year. We got fifteen gallons less juice out of the grapes than normal. But every drop counts. Cheers!" The perfect mix of the Okanagan light and the deep wood tones and baritones of Alsace.

Cases of empty wine bottles fill every corner of the kitchen, and we will spend three hours bottling this wine and corking it, but right then we raise our glasses against the naked electric bulb. The light splashes through them like a wind, and we clink the glasses together.

This is the wine I took to Toronto.

To get that wine to Toronto, I drove off the plateau on the long curl past the diseased pines and house trailers above Horse Lake. This was the path of the voyageurs, and you can still buy a trapline there, for five thousand bucks. Cheap. From that you can expect an annual income of around $187.

I slipped down off the escarpment on a muddy gravel road, slick with clay, to the sand banks and hollow cottonwoods of the Thompson River at Little Fort. At Barriere, a big red sign towered above the junked cars and broken-down chicken wire and ten-year-old pale brown cornstalks of an old hippy encampment: OUR RIVERS ARE NOT FOR SALE: DAM FREE TRADE. There, beside that river where the Overlanders drowned a hundred and forty years ago as the rapids and whirlpools swallowed their cattle and their chickens and broke up their rafts, I drove in an old rusty pickup, south to the old railway town of Kamloops. Kamloops stinks. There is no pretty way to talk about Kamloops: in the sagebrush and bunchgrass, the steam and sulphur dioxide pours out of the smokestack of the pulp mill. It rises in a high white plume, straight up above the airport, like a searchlight beaming into the sky. As it cools in the air it grows white and thick. Later it sinks back over the city, invisible, and smells like rotten eggs. This is the worst part of the journey – close to home.

We took off from Kamloops in an eighteen-seat Jet-stream. This is the kind of plane where the captain himself loads your bags and shows you to your seat. Everyone has a window seat and a clear view to the instruments in the cockpit, too. Immediately after take-off we banked hard over the sewage ponds and the lily-green water of the river. Within two minutes we lost the river and the mountains in puffy low cloud. "God," said a man across the aisle – a tall guy, forty, with cool, easy manners and a wind-burnt face. He wore a checked Indonesian flannel shirt: red and blue and black. "I hope we weren't following the river."

"Don't worry. There are lots more rivers. We're bound to find one sooner or later." I didn't bother telling him that they all flowed north-south – no use to us. It was not a storm, however, only low fog forming on the river for two hundred miles as it cooled in the fall and collected against the temperature inversion of Kamloops. We were soon out of it and flew in white sunlight over mountains, clearcuts, glaciers, and high, green alpine tarns. They lay below us, sparkling in the intense light like paint discs in a child's paint set. By the time the dams and reservoirs of the Columbia fell behind us, the peaks of the Rockies were only a few feet below the plane, in a pure blue sky. The colour was so clean it was as if we had entered an eye. The air was the sun. This was where the earth and the sun touched and became each other. It was obvious. I wondered why I had never seen that before. Fog was forming off the faces of the farthest peaks, streaming east. The light was so intense, I expected to see an angel sitting on the plane's wing. As I watched the sun sparkle on the wingtip, the mountains stopped abruptly and the earth fell away below, a glowing gold. We landed amid the brown fields of Calgary, each with its small tin hut and black oil pump. Cattle grazed in industrial gravel, tearing up weeds. The sun burned just a few inches over the soil.

There was no going back.

The flight to Toronto severed my mind neatly in two: painless surgery. The results were startling. As we drove in from the airport, one half of my mind was spinning wildly through the city at breakneck speed, flashing between looming shadows and gleaming lights. The other half was talking slowly, measuredly, to Maria. I explained to her what *Iodine* was about – a little late perhaps, but there had been things about the book which I had wanted to keep hidden – most importantly, that the book was the story of a real man: Eric, or Dogman as he was known in the Similkameen. To anger Eric would be to set loose an unpredictable and conceivably violent sequence of events. I didn't think he'd find me in Toronto, though. I figured it was safe to talk, at last. In stereo.

Eric came to the valley in the winter of 1974, when he was thirty years old, with a graduate degree in psychology. That winter he took an apple tree pruning course on our farm. Six foot two inches tall, broad-shouldered, black-bearded, and wearing the pair of mechanic's overalls he was to wear for the next twenty years, he spoke haltingly and with his eyes averted – looking anywhere else but at his listener – about psychology and politics. Every word he spoke was measured, as if there was an intense fire he was compressing within it by an act of his will alone. It was hard work for him – his face was strained as he talked – but he did it. He was still social then. For two years he pruned in the orchards. After that, the effort became too much. The next sixteen years he spent in an eighty-year-old mineshaft above the valley. For company he had thirty dogs that he had stolen one at a time from the farmers below. After a decade, the SPCA came and put them down, except for six, which they said he could care for. Well, I've seen what they used at the pound in Penticton when they killed dogs: a black pistol, which you held against a dog's skull; when you pull the trigger a spring-loaded four-inch steel piston smashes deep into the dog's brain. "I can't use this," the poundkeeper had said that day, throwing it across the desk. "I'm quitting." I bought the desk: solid oak; thirty bucks. I'm writing on it.

Eric's life on the mountain became the subject of legend and derision. Few people had met Eric, yet everyone had a story about him. I was one of the few who *had* met him, and I got to thinking that if he had lived five hundred years ago he would have been called a saint, a positive rather than a negative deviation from social norms. I was young. I understood idealism. It made sense to me. I would look up at Fairview Mountain, knowing that Eric was there, and knowing that he had entered the land; for him there were no more compromises. My life in the valley below was fraught with compromises – between art, which I had learned in the city, and farming, which I had learned on that land. I was trying to bring them together. It grew harder and harder to take myself seriously, however, and one day as I stared up at the blue-and-white shoulder of that mountain, I realized that with his long, tangled, dark hair, set face, wild eyes, and black beard, Eric looked a lot like the pictures of Jesus I had grown up with.

I got to thinking. "You know, if man is created in God's image, then He's all around us here." Bunchgrass, fallen barbed wire, rusted pickups, old fridges turned into fruit dryers then kicked over under the lilacs and forgotten. "After two thousand years of trying to make the land into His image, this life is what we've rigged together. Not much, perhaps, but the best city of cut crystal we could build. After all, we are only human!" So I sang it. I sang it with Texaco brake fluid, Roundup herbicide, Campbell's soup, Stimula ribbed condoms, gas barbecues, and Colombian coffee. I sang about paradise on earth. I sang the poem that counts. I discovered the power of forgiveness and praise. Everything was alright.

In Toronto I was less certain. With homemade wine, uncertainty is usually best. Over the years I've had wine – Brian's – that tasted like gun cleaner, heady brown port that sent tears of alcohol beading on the glass, poison that had oxidized to a deep brown. That stuff was like drinking a headache out of a bottle. One sip of that and it squeezed your temples with a C-clamp and would not let go. "Ah," said fior, a Ministry of Highways mechanic in the mountain city of Nelson, about that one. It had been aged in an old rye whiskey barrel, and it tasted like it too. Fior sat around with his Italian father and his friends and his father's friends, in a circle on folding chairs next to the laundry tubs in his basement, with a box of Tide on the shelf above them, and passed around the jug. "That one's a keeper," fior said, smacking his lips. Everyone nodded appreciatively, gravely. Some farmers just give up and pass a bottle of ginger ale over when they slide a bottle of their wine to you. "I like to mix them," they say. "I like wine that way." When a farmer says that, do it. It's good advice. Don't argue.

I must have touched a nerve. I have friends who are devout Christians. Paul, for instance, son of a Lutheran pastor in Kelowna, and a customs inspector who likes to "joke" that he is "protecting the homeland," laughed out loud when he read my book, then looked up troubled, and pale, from his living room couch, while our children played with video games in the next room. "This is heresy," he said.

"I don't get it," I answered back. "Would you prefer to be dismissed altogether? Is that what Christians want?"

"They are old people mostly," Paul said, apologetically, but firmly, too. "People come to the church for comfort and tradition. Not to think. That is precisely not why they are there."

There were not many stars above the airport as Maria and I walked through the yellow sodium night to the parking lot. It wasn't like sitting with my daughter a week before in the lawn chairs on my gravel driveway in the Cariboo with a flashlight and a book as the frost settled around us on the cabbages. In that black cold there had been so many stars I had felt I was floating in an ancient shaman's dream on the gravel shore of a Siberian river as leafless silver birches shivered above him. Blue, orange, yellow, and steel-white, there were so many stars that our star charts were nearly useless: after half an hour our fingers were frozen, yet out of the white flood we had only deciphered the shapes of Cygnus and Pisces and the Pleiades. As I had shone the flashlight up to point out stars to my daughter, the beam of the light had streamed above us, reflecting off tiny ice crystals in the air.

Above the Toronto airport, I saw Orion clearly, easily, burning through the city as the city reflected itself as a white sheet through the entire bulk of the air: unwavering and still. But I saw no other stars. The air was liquid, and it was very old. In the Cariboo the air hadn't been old at all: it looked as if it was being made just then.

As Maria and I drove away from the airport and deeper into the city, the high-rises and the life insurance towers and the big blue Warner Brothers Building rose up into the yellow night: perfect grids. They floated past, looking just as the city itself had looked from ten thousand feet: a glowing, white-hot chainlink fence. It was a world perfectly formed. All around us traffic streamed in a ribbon of liquid steel – a bright spark spilling out of a Candu reactor into the night. The city was a huge art installation: it was like when Christo wrapped the coast of California – the live-oak hills – in white cloth, back in the seventies, for mile on mile on mile.

Who says you can't travel in time?

3

READING

OUT LOUD

A month before I flew to Toronto, Maria and Heather had phoned to ask who I wanted to invite to my reading. "Peter!" Diane had called from the kitchen table, where she was marking Grade 9 math tests: answers scribbled down by skateboarders, jocks, and farm kids to whom algebra was a secret and puzzling language. I had laughed again. Peter! Of course! Peter Gzowski. It would be great to have him there.

Now, I should tell you a little about my relationship with Peter. For us who lived in the bunchgrass and pine mountains of British Columbia in those years, Peter was Canada. He was family. I mean, we had heard him learn to tie a tie, after all – and how to iron a shirt, how to cook crepes, even how to waltz. When we listened to Peter we believed that the idea of Canada worked: in the same way that the bighorn sheep scattered down the dykes, drank the cool willow-water, then skittered back up the talus cones and purple basalt mountains, we listened to Peter. When he said "Good-bye" and it was time for the news, we switched to American country-and-western radio and its songs of plastic loss and pain, blasted out of the transmitters in Spokane to the Fairchild air base among the ponderosas and sagebrush hills. The hay flew out of the backs of our pickups as we drove home for lunch: fragrant clouds.

Three springs ago, as the yellow-headed blackbirds stole every wheat seed out of my garden, flashing for days on the bare, dark soil, I thought of Peter, in Toronto, in Canada. He seemed so far away. I thought he'd like those birds too, so I made a tape to send to him. *I had a farm in Cawston*, I spoke into the microphone. I was standing in front of the window, staring over the lake. The glass pulsed faintly with the booming of bitterns and the shrieks of coots, grebes, mallards, goldeneyes, geese, mergansers, teal, buffleheads, and loons –

mating on the black spring water. It was only a week since the ice had broken up. The mornings were full of fog. I was echoing Karen Blixen in Kenya: *at the foot of the Fairview Hills. The border runs through this country, about fifteen miles to the South. In the daytime you felt that the sun and the earth had become one world, but the mornings and evenings were cool and windy, and the nights were cold.* I talked about a lot of things: about the Industrial Revolution and five generations struggling to get back to the land; about the wind; about sheep being fed two pounds of DDT a day to cure worms; about my cousin Hans, whose whole life was spent on the railroad work gangs out of Kamloops – not a whole lot better than prison. But I never sent it.

For a decade I'd worked with Peter on Robert Mennell's orchard in Cawston, pruning Red Delicious apple trees. Robert had wired a fourteen-inch speaker to the radio of his rusty Ford Courier pickup. He'd set the speaker on the roof and would turn the volume up so loud we could hear Peter above our chainsaws and our laughter and the steady click-click of our clippers and the dull groaning of our polesaws. For ten years I worked there in Peter's voice, as he swam slowly, ethereal, among the bare, grey branches.

One spring day as we grafted pear trees there with Peter, we heard the sandhill cranes lift off from the flooded hayfields across the highway. For four days we had worked in their low trumpeting – a huge flock of two hundred and fifty birds that had come down for shelter to the marshes of the flooded pastures and hayfields, and which had been trapped there as snow fell from the floor of the clouds. They huddled in the thin water, calling like clay horns, as slow, cold squawfish swam around their feet. Over those days we had grown used to these birds, which are usually only high, tattered vees in the strong winds a mile above the valley. On the day they lifted off, we stood in the middle of the road, a small, raggedly dressed group, our clothes stained with chain oil, two-cycle gas, sawdust, and grafting paint, still wearing

our safety goggles: five Groucho Marxes lined up in a row.
First one bird lifted off, slowly, from the reflected swirls and
puddles of the sky, then another bird, and another, and
another: four birds, slowly climbing in a spiralling, ever-
widening cone. As the trumpeting grew louder and louder, a
few more birds lifted off, sometimes singly and sometimes in
groups of ten, circled above the flock, then settled down
again. Then another cluster would rise up and settle down.
Then the trumpeting grew deafening. A thin column of birds
climbed out of the field, spiralling in a long, swinging arc.
One by one, other birds joined it, until the whole flock was in
the air, a huge, long dark line. Within two minutes the flock
had risen to seven thousand feet and was sweeping in a wide
circle the width of the valley. Then the lead birds swung due
north and the others followed: a tattered vee, small at that
height. Their trumpeting drifted down over us, ripped and
broken up by the wind. In all that sound we lost Peter altogether. We stood there for five minutes, then the cranes were
gone, over the blue shoulder of Apex Mountain. Only slowly
did we come back to ourselves, in the silence and stillness, on
the gravel of the roadside, and realize that Peter was still talking to us softly among the trees.

During that decade we all learned to sing of our country
because no other songs would fit – the c&w eight-tracks on
the dash had grown boring from overuse and the classics
seemed foreign and lifeless – but while Peter was singing of
Canada, in Toronto, early in the morning, I learned to sing of
a valley of soapstone and shale, drenched with moonlight
and the gritty winds of the sun. Were we talking about the
same thing? I don't know. That is the question that struck me
again and again in Toronto. I stood there in the middle of the
black stage of the Palmerston Public Library and looked for
Peter in the crowd. He wasn't there. His voice didn't echo as
a background shadow around the feet of the people there, or
even as a screech of feedback in the mike. I read without him.
But then, I'm used to that. I drove all the way to Victoria

once, to read. My payment was a quiet dinner, one woman walking out after I read from my manuscript *Iodine*, and an excruciating and noisy hour in a pub where I couldn't hear anything anyone said. Hardly anyone had come to the reading: Peter was in town.

I read with Ethel Harris. Ethel read *A Rage of Poppies*: chiselled, human affirmations gained from a life of pain and loss, sandwiched between blood-red endpapers.

"I love the red paper," I said. I did.

Dave from the University of Toronto Bookstore was trying to figure out which jack to plug the mike into: "I always get these things wrong," he said, bending over and peering at the back of the amp.

I declaimed Shakespeare, "Let me not to the marriage of true minds admit impediments," to the half-empty hall. The mike was dead.

Ethel kept asking, "Do I have to use this? I don't really want to. I don't want to use it. I'll knock it over. Do I have to use it? They'll hear me. It's not so big here. I don't want to use it."

"Donne!" someone called from the back.

"Try that," said Dave, shoving the jacks into different sockets in the back of the amp.

"Love is not love that alters when it alteration finds, or bends with the remover to remove ... How does that sound?"

"Great!" someone called from the back.

"Marvell!" someone else called.

I stepped away from the mike and shrugged. "No you don't," I said to Ethel. "It doesn't matter."

"Good," she said. "I don't want to."

She read strongly. A mike would have been completely the wrong thing. She was intimate. Her timing was perfect.

Ethel's last poem was a dream for a dove: a sacred redemption, an image of atonement and grace. There, as she read in the library basement, it was as if an Old Testament God had walked into the room with us. We were surrounded by Him, but couldn't see Him. As He breathed, we breathed. That's how He keeps hidden. Our skin tingled. And then – after the applause at this invocation, like when a magician pulls doves out of a deep, black hat and lets them fly up off the tips of his fingers, when you know for sure that it was not a trick – I read a poem to that God: *Dad*, I said. *We're tired of books without pictures. We love the* NATIONAL GEOGRAPHIC. *We need an afternoon nap.* The air snapped and went still – tensed like a cat waiting to spring on a mouse. As I looked out at the audience, I realized that I was a long, long way from home. I was Sinbad, in that old book I had as a kid, the one with the embossed leather cover and in which the pictures were inserted between the signatures at random: they had nothing to do with the story you were reading at all. A giant bird had carried me off and dropped me in a land of gold and precious gems.

Ethel's audience sat there in the half dark, and I read to them, across all that distance, and I read through them to the still and crackling air, *Iodine*, an attempt to remake for our time through the myth of creative transformation the cycle of death and birth that grounds Christian sacred traditions. I was a little uncertain, to say the least. I read for twenty minutes. By the end everyone was laughing right along. And there I closed with the sad but true story of going to an auto wrecker in Penticton and watching the mechanics break the last used Volvo brake rotor in BC and Alberta as they tried to get it off by brute force alone.

Just remember, I read.
The blue-suited mechanics
who work at the wrecking yard,
sitting around drinking coffee
until you come in
looking for a brake rotor,
are working there
and not at the garage down the street
for a reason. You didn't
after all expect poetry to live in a vacuum,
did you?

After I read, the audience walked slowly up to the stage, in no particular order, relaxed, as if they were walking in a procession. Once onstage, they drifted more quickly, then broke up and elbowed their way into the crackers, cheese, and wine spread out along the black stage wall. They ate as if they hadn't eaten in weeks. They carried the food away so carefully in their hands, slowing down more and more the farther they went from the tables. I was left to drink wine and to talk to a poet from the sixties who had turned to writing science fiction.

"That's all I ever read anyway," he said. "I'm tired of all the garbage in the literary magazines." He couldn't believe that I had never been to Toronto. He took a big mouthful of wine and swallowed it all at once. "Everyone's been to Toronto." He smiled crookedly and peered through his one-quarter-inch-thick glasses to try and get a look at me.

Maria and I drove home through the black trees of the Toronto night. They raged around us like big sleeping sheep. The lights of the traffic flickered over our faces.

S omeday you'll be a poet," says my friend Alex. Alex lives in a pine forest in the Cariboo, in unceasing pain as tumours in his neck press on his spinal cord and the stem of his brain – tumours that came from the beatings the police gave him with a metal pipe in Santiago in 1973. Alex's house is falling down around him. The fence is collapsing into the weeds. The sundeck is falling away. He tore the railing off the front steps to get a piano in four years ago: it hasn't been replaced. A neon-pink sign, a metre long, greets you as you come in the door: LOVE EACH OTHER.

Alex has given up on the church. "God saved me from my pain," he says. "But not the church." Alex has taught himself Latin, Greek, and Hebrew and has formed, out of fitful reading, his own religion. He teaches his family in it every day. For Alex, life is an intrigue; love is a duty. "You don't know what I have been doing for you," he says. "People say, 'Harold's a heretic. What are we going to do about him?' and I tell them 'Be patient, he'll be a poet someday.' You need to write these stories just as they are. Look at *this* poem. Why do you have Christ imitating Elvis and standing on a car hoist at Canadian Tire? Christ would never imitate Elvis. Christ was the greatest man who ever lived. If he came to the world today, I would follow him. I would leave my family right away and go with him, wherever he went. You have to follow a man like that. He would not need to imitate Elvis. Elvis would imitate him."

"But it's the same thing," I say. "It's a metaphor. It's about yearning. It's about reverence. Look, it ends with the lines *Love Me Tender! Love Me True!*"

"Don't get me wrong," says Alex. "I think it's really funny. But it *is* heresy."

I couldn't say a thing. I thought you couldn't use that word anymore. I thought it had died out with the black plague.

"How do you think people feel when you write like this?" he went on. "It hurts people."

finally I found the words. "But it hurts *me* when you call it heresy! Nobody goes to church anymore. Don't you think there's a reason for that?"

"Around here they do. Lots of them. You have to write about real people. You can write like Neruda. You should." His voice went quiet. "I met Neruda. He came to our biology class. It was an anatomy class. We were dissecting corpses. He asked us intelligent questions. Most people who came were stupid. He watched. He didn't say anything, then he asked thoughtful questions about the structure of the muscles in the face. He understood things. He could see patterns. He was always thinking. He was one of us. The government persecuted him for years, you know. They broke into his house and smashed all his books. I heard him read. He wore a red beret and a black cape. He swirled the cape at the end of a poem and turned away. At the last word he looked back over his shoulder like a matador and spoke, deadpan. It was so dramatic. He was our brother. Then the police came and beat us. Those kinds of men are stupid. All my friends were killed. I saw their bodies lined up, lying in the street. I got out, working in the engine room of a Greek freighter. Straight from university to the grease: you can't imagine. One day, classes, the next day, the engine room. That's it. The engines were unmuffled. The Greeks didn't care about us. We were slaves. They didn't give us earplugs. We had to sleep among the engines. It was so damp and cold. Our clothes turned green and rotted off us. The engines stank. You could hardly breathe. All your skin stank of diesel, for a long time. The engines were so loud we couldn't hear for two weeks after that. I came to Canada: it was a silent country. No one made a sound. No one gave me coffee. I was invisible. My skin smelled of diesel oil for months. Don't attack the founder of a religion. Attack the church."

The next day, Heather and I went looking for a red tree. On the bank of a river crusted with frost-withered sumacs and running over a bed of broken sidewalks and smashed concrete sewer pipes and twisted metal we found one orange tree.

"Oh no!" Heather said, as we stood and stared at the otherwise green wall of the ravine. "It was at its prime a few days ago." We walked farther. "Harold," Heather said at last. "I'm sorry. It's the best we're going to find." We'd been walking for an hour and we'd come full circle. We stopped and stared at the orange tree. It was a glorious shade of orange, to be sure, and right then and there I had a vision. I dreamed of changing the colour of the flag, a different colour for every season: white for winter, blue for spring, green for summer, orange for fall. There could be special ceremonies for changing it, like laying a wreath on a cenotaph. Heather sighed. "You see, the colours haven't started to change here in the city yet. We haven't had a frost. We'll have to get out of the city if we're going to see red trees."

But of course, you can't get out of the city by car or by foot. You can only get out of the city if you fly. It is a city of dreams.

In this dream, young women jog in pairs through the university grounds. A fifty-year-old man in a Toronto Blue Jays sweater, with a rough, uncombed ponytail hanging from his backwards-turned baseball cap, rides an old ten-speed bicycle with sun-faded paint, very quickly, as if he is late for a costume party in Wonderland. I turn to look after him, once he has passed. He is just rounding a corner on the gravel path by the river. He is hunched over the handlebars. No watch hangs out of the back pocket of his cutoff jeans. Just as quickly, he is gone.

In this dream, orange flotation rings and long curved metal poles hang on posts along a shallow river. The water looks like aluminum. Signs are posted, in black and white, among the sumacs: NO SWIMMING. DANGEROUS CURRENTS. ABSOLUTELY NO SWIMMING: WATER POLLUTED.

"You should see this river in the spring," a woman says in this dream. "It is very high. There is nothing here but water. Now look at it. That's the way it is with rivers in Ontario."

That is the way it is with rivers everywhere.

The Blue Jay comes riding back, sweating, fast. He pumps up a muddy hill and whizzes by, brushing my sleeve.

Years after Wayne and my wife Diane and I had met on his farm, Brian Mennell and I sat in his living room with glasses of red wine. The wine hovered in the glasses like the water in a spirit level. It tasted like a whole summer of leaves gently turning over and under in the light. It was the sun recorded, moment by moment, through the medium of the leaves.

"Our education in Keremeos was useless," said Brian. "I didn't learn anything at school. A third of us dropped out. You write poetry. It's all a failure of education. Don't get me wrong. I'd never read that stuff. I have a hard time even reading a newspaper. It's OK by me, but it's just that you can't write anything that is of use to this valley and can be read by the people of this valley. So your education has failed you. It has failed all of us."

"But that's what I try to do," I said. "Someone has to talk about these things. We squeeze more and more people into a ninety-year-old agricultural subdivision. The farms are being wrecked. The town is being wrecked, while ninety-five percent of the area belongs to the Crown: inaccessible. Nobody knows what's going on there. No one's responsible for it. We should build towns *there*. Look at the mess up Easygoing Creek: it's a clearcut! Gorman Brothers: that's ninety miles away. Those are Keremeos trees, but they were hauled to Westbank. The replanted trees are all dead. We need land reform. Like in the Philippines."

"That's just my point," said Brian, reaching for a bottle. The record of his winemaking was written with pencil on a strip of masking tape on the bottle's green shoulder: Brix at harvest; ppm. sulphur. No pretense. He filled my glass again. "You do it in poetry. No one reads poetry."

"Maybe I can change that."

"Nobody will change that. Maybe we should all read poetry, but we won't. It's too much work. It's that simple. No one has the time."

I swallowed a mouthful of red light. It poured through my veins. I was a flower.

Outside, the snow sifted around the house.

"Well now, that's depressing."

"No, it's not," he said, grinning.

Like the Cheshire cat.

For the first generation here, the land was something to be cut up and plowed, seeded and planted. To Brian, Robert, and me, however, who grew into a culture already formed and with at least the outward appearance of stability and solidity, there was a choice between immediacy and abstraction. On the one hand stood land and art – apple tastings in late October, coffee breaks in the afternoon, wine-making in the basement, and politics, everywhere, at all times – in short, the life of a country gentleman. On the other side stood the sale of that land for cash, and through that cash the achievement of that image, but without the work to attain it and without the land to bend it, always, deep into the earth, to always temper the books, the art, the wine, our houses, and our thought. When Brian spoke to me that day, his analysis was exactly right: there was no way I could continue to write among the orchards without making any connection to the people of the valley, not through farming but through writing.

"If I write about the valley, it's no different from what anybody else writes," I said. "They should read that in Toronto."

"It shouldn't make a difference. But it does." He was firm.

And he was right.

Welcome to the Third World.

The more Canada succeeded as an industrial country, and the higher our dollar went in value, the worse-off the farmers in the Similkameen became, because our markets were in the US, the Far East, and Europe, and our competitors – Mexico, Chile, Turkey, Brazil – had no standard of living at all. We had been poor like that once, but we were poor no more, and we were no longer of use.

Similarly, for year after year after year we sent our young people off to receive a university education in Vancouver and

Victoria, and with hardly any exceptions they stayed there. Without the energy of the young and the cultural inheritance they represent, the valley has little intellectual, spiritual, and cultural continuity in time and development through time; it has only real estate development – the marketing and sale of images of our culture: picture postcards, the plate glass window of a five-thousand-square-foot Tudor house with a view down over subdivided old orchards. It is a culture stunted at an oral, subjugated level. That is the paradox and the tragedy of our time: in the middle of a vast silence – all of our lives that we might have learned to speak – the Okanagan and Similkameen have become an article in a travel magazine.

The farm I had dreamed of never materialized. Farming was deteriorating as a way of life. When my daughter was old enough to go to school, I discovered I had friends who wanted the school system to shelter their children from academic challenge. It was a sobering blow. At the same time, farmers were struggling more every year. In the Okanagan, just a few miles over the mountains, farming had already almost vanished. Twenty years ago, farmers wanted to be protected by legislation. Now they put up billboards along the highways: BUY BC FRUIT: SAVE OUR FAMILY FARM, with a bunch of grandkids and a granddad and a happy mom and dad in bright clothes. The suburbs grow.

Seven years ago, just before leaving the Similkameen for wilder earth, I sat with Brian and a few friends around a glowing fire on the edge of Empire Orchards in Keremeos – five generations rooted to the stony Similkameen land – and said good-bye. As the sun thinned, draining leaf-green out of the sky, one broad streak of cloud boiled out of the Cathedrals, towered, rising upon itself, sinking down, catching the last jewelled white-water brightness from the air. The air was the last leaf-glint of summer. Against it, we watched crows pass overhead, silent, one at a time, in a falling wind. By the time the last flew by, a mile behind its fellows, happy, in that perennial stand-up comedy which is the life of crows, we were standing in a half-circle, drinks in hand, facing south – and only then were we aware it was dark and the first stars had been shining for a long time.

When I arrived in the Cariboo, I stepped down out of the truck. I was so buoyed up, the aspens seemed to laugh, like dogs, crowding around my legs in their joy to see me home, like children, like very wise, ancient children, who need love if they are to survive this time, the time of reckoning.

The next summer I returned to the Similkameen to get some flowers for my garden in the Cariboo. I went to John Bibby, direct descendant of one of the Overlanders who *didn't* drown in the rapids of the Thompson River.

"I quit school in the Depression," says John, as we sip perc coffee in his trailer looking over his big vegetable garden. "There were no jobs anywhere. I had ridden the rails to Vancouver and was chased by the railway cops. There was nothing there, either. All us young men lay flat on the tops of boxcars, with the smoke in our eyes and the darkness of the tunnels. I remember one fellow who didn't lie flat in time. He just ran flat into the face of a tunnel and was gone." After a summer at Douglas Lake, the 100,000-acre cattle ranch in the bunchgrass hills between Kamloops and Merritt, John's luck changed. "My father died," he said, "which made me the man of the house. I had to look after my family, but I also inherited some money – $18,000. I knew I had better not squander it, so I used it to buy an orchard in Naramata. That was in 1936. I kept that orchard until 1949, when I could not stand it anymore and sold out."

We had finished our coffee by this point and were out digging irises in John's front yard, with the bittersweet taste of coffee whitener on our tongues. The floodplain of the Similkameen River spread out at the bottom of the hill below us, a wide expanse of swamps, willowbrakes, and the pastures of the old Richter Ranch. Ten years previously, John had bought a few iris plants. They thrived on his hill of cactus and sand. Around us as we dug that day in the August sun, a half acre of flowers bloomed in long rows. John gave them away profusely, but they still multiplied more quickly than he could handle.

"All through the war," said John, "we got good prices for

our apples. There were price controls. We did very well. We got the same price as we did in the 1970s. But I couldn't stand it anymore."

I had lived beside John's old orchard as it tumbled down the clay banks in Naramata, from the mountain to the lake, swaying up and down the sides of a clay gully like a canoe caught in rapids. I couldn't imagine getting any closer to paradise, with the apricot trees growing among the ponderosa pines and the sage.

"Couldn't stand what?" I asked, puzzled.

A bumblebee tumbled into a six-inch scarlet bloom in front of me. For a moment the flower trembled violently, then the bee buzzed out again, with a roar like a military transport plane. It was hot.

"I couldn't stand to pay my workers so little," said John, wiping a trickle of sweat off his forehead. "I sold the place and moved to Vancouver."

As we dug up samples of every colour from seed catalogues, friends, and even ones John had bred himself, I heard how that hadn't worked out either. John had divorced his wife as well, but in Vancouver he let her continue to live with him.

"It was terrible," he said. "We really hated each other, but I felt sorry for her. She had no means of support and I felt responsible."

After twenty penniless years in the rain, John moved back to the Okanagan, specifically to Similkameen Station, where he bought the old Andrés Wines vineyard for a song and nursed it along for a decade on the work of his hands alone. Andrés, a Port Moody winery, set up among the train tracks and oil refineries to sell mostly jug wines from California grapes, planted the vineyard to maintain Canadian production quotas, which in turn allowed it to produce its highly lucrative, palate-searing products. The vineyard nearly bankrupted Andrés. In the 1960s, before widespread use of weed-killers, Andrés was expending huge sums of money to have the entire thirty acres hoed weekly by hand. John made it work on the thrift he had learned in Naramata. He hardly spent a cent.

Despite his eternal optimism, John seemed to carry his own private Depression within him like the refrain to a song. A year after he sold the vineyard to Brian – but kept his trailer and garden – all the grapes died in the winter cold, except for four acres on the higher ground of alluvial shale and soapstone that had fallen off the mountain and had been deposited there by flash floods – the topsoil two feet below the surface of the soil. His garden of brilliant irises was surrounded by a forty-acre field of two-foot-high dandelions, white in the moonlight, and a sea of weathered cedar posts.

It was best not to talk to John about that.

"Poetry is a luxury we can't afford," said John to me that year, when I was living among those dandelions and posts, working with Brian to recover something of the vineyard. "All art is a luxury." The world was drenched with the rain of an unusually wet spring – Wayne and I joked that if we had wanted weather like this we would have moved to Vancouver long before. The puffy dandelion seedheads were ragged with rain and most of them were stripped of their seeds.

The winter after John and I dug irises on that August day, he died – eighty-two years old. In our last act together, he had given me his entire iris collection for safekeeping, all thirty different colours, including the rare ones he had never shared with me before. I moved them to the Cariboo.

"I'm giving you this one, too," he said that day. "It's called Ming Dynasty. It's supposed to be butterscotch-coloured, with fine brown lines on the petals, but on this soil it comes out without any lines at all. I'll give it to you to see if it will do any differently in your soil."

As we dug the plants together and loaded them into plastic bags and into the back of my pickup, I sensed immediately the weight of the trust John had given to me – that he wanted something of his life – a life on the land – to continue, in a world that seemed to have passed it completely by. Now the irises grow among the bull thistles in my garden, and the rich, heavy blooms hum with bumblebees among the calls of loons, a wind off a plateau lake, and the incessant creaking *scree-scree* of the blackbirds in the reedbeds.

"I rarely get any seeds," John had said, "because they need a big insect, like a bumblebee, to pollinate them, but we have mostly honeybees here." Up in the Cariboo there are no honeybees, but plenty of bumblebees. Ming Dynasty has fine brown lines. I have no farm.

4

STREET

WISE

I had decided not to go into Toronto unprepared. My brother Roland lived for twelve years in Belleville. He knew Toronto well. For information, he was a good man to start with. Belleville I knew a bit, from the poems of Al Purdy: a land of poor soil, rocks, abandoned farmsteads, contour plowing *that became the convolutions of one's own brain,* as Purdy put it in his poem "The Country North of Belleville," and agricultural dreams that made us Canadians before they broke and were abandoned. Purdy obviously felt drawn to them too, and out of his struggle with them he hacked out an individual, human voice: like the first settlers chopping farms out of the moraines with an axe, a pry-bar, and a horse. As good a kind of poetry as any – and scarcely different from our work in the Interior, either. My brother knew Belleville as a small, boring city with no economy. That's all he ever said about it, except, offhand, that as the transportation and trading hub for the old rural hinterland, it is the perfect setting for a modern industrial plant – outside of the expense of the city but linked to it closely, and with a willing workforce because there was nothing else there for them to do.

Roland worked in Belleville as a managing engineer for Proctor and Gamble: this kid who drove the farm tractors when he was nine years old, taught himself to weld aluminum – a difficult art, because the stuff tends to melt away from you and bubble like an Aero bar and not knit together – when he was twelve, and crashed eleven vehicles when he was sixteen, including his single-piston Norton Gold Star 500cc bike, the engine of which fell out of the frame at 110 MPH outside of Similkameen Station in a stream of sparks like a comet behind him in the night. He had a vision, though. He left town in Grade 11, boarded in a rooming house in Kelowna, got a decent high-school education, and went to the best engineering school in North America: Purdue, in Lafayette, Indiana, USA. We used to make a lot of jokes in the family about Roland's industrial aspirations. So often in those years I pictured him talking to other aspiring executives on one of his many business trips. "I'm in electronics," the fellow in the seat next to him in business class would say, squeezing the lime into his gin and tonic. "What line are you in?" "Pampers," my brother would say, tipping a beer up to his lips, his eyes sparkling. "Ya," my dad laughed about it. "You could say he's started at the *bottom!*"

"I like to get downtown only about once a month," Roland once told me. "So I wouldn't mind living in a suburb. I couldn't farm anymore. I've finally given that up."

"Why?" I'd asked. This was an important question to me, too. I was looking for answers.

"I couldn't farm unless I could be the best there is. You can't do that in Canada. It's all so small-scale. It's out of date. It's so fucking Mickey Mouse." We were remembering our lives as kids on the farm – that big, sprawling, sixties farm, politically, horticulturally, technically, and chemically one of the foremost in the country – and about how it felt to be cut off from that life. I had faced the same sense of loss by working to recreate the social and spiritual values we had known there. But then, while I was pruning the trees as saw-whet owls hunted around me, Roland was in the shed, tearing down the engine of a Massey Ferguson tractor: it was the technical value he was attempting to recreate. We were like Olympic athletes: our careers were over by the time we were eighteen. The adjustment was hard. The task that faced both of us was to find a way to carry forward what we had learned, there where Czech and Japanese scientists had come to walk and learn among the trees and where we pioneered the use of growth hormones – growth and crop regulators which eventually became the infamous Alar. It seems that once you heat it, to pasteurize it, in juice, it's a bit carcinogenic. Oh well. We tried – we had one entire orchard block devoted to testing Alar, in which each tree was a different size and shape, some rich with blossoms, some without an apple at all, some with a thousand tiny branches, some tall, thin, and branchless, some with roots, leaves, bark, and even small twigs growing from the skin of the fruit. Roland had obviously made his peace with Alar, but I still thought his comment a little strange: Belleville didn't sound like such a big town to me. So I asked further. "Downtown?"

"Toronto, of course."

What had been strange had become even stranger yet. I had looked at maps. Ontario was *big*. "You mean to say that for all of Southern Ontario, Toronto is downtown?"

"You bet," he said. He laughed.

It is the end of the earth.

This time I phoned Roland in Cincinnati. With the signing of the Free Trade pact, management had been radically cut out of P&G Canada. He hadn't even hesitated to move. "I should never have come back to Canada after university," he explained. "When I went to Purdue, they thought I was American. When I crossed over the border with my student visa, they didn't know what to make of me. They thought BC was in Central America! 'No,' I told them. 'It's north of Washington State.' 'Washington *what*? Where's that?' 'By California.' 'But this isn't an American drivers' license.' It was hopeless. When I moved to Belleville, everyone thought I was a Yank. Now that I'm in Cincinnati, they think I'm a Yank too. It's fate!"

I was getting smarter. I didn't hesitate either. I didn't ask about downtown.

W hat's there to do in Toronto?" I asked.
"Geez," Roland answered. "If I wasn't in the process
of getting my green card, I'd come up and see you. I'd show
you the town! But I can't leave the country for six months.
Football, baseball, hockey, what else? Hmmm … Chinatown!
It's a different world. The CN Tower on a clear day."

"Do I have to?" I interjected on the phone, suddenly.

"You have to." He chuckled. "But only just to see how big
the whole area is. The market – some of the ethnic neigh-
bourhoods. Make sure you do that. But not at night. Don't
go there at night. Try the subway. It even works! But be careful at night. Be street smart: just the normal sort of thing.
What you would do anywhere. Keep your money and your
credit cards and your ID split up. Put it in four or five different place. That way, when you get mugged you have something left. You can carry on your life normally."

Four or five different places! How many times was I supposed to get mugged in one night? I went out and bought a
second wallet, a very thin one. I had been using a large hand
wallet for a year: my previous wallet, carried on my hip, had
given me terrible back pain. But for Toronto, I'd endure a bit
of pain in my back.

The week that I was in Toronto I had crumpled, sweaty
$20 bills in my pockets, but it just didn't seem like I had done
enough. I couldn't help thinking I was meant to stuff more
bills down my socks. I kept my eyes open. No one looked like
they had money stuffed down their socks. No one walked
stiffly. No one limped either, for that matter: there were no
signs of money anywhere.

Almost everyone in Toronto wore a leather jacket. Out on the farm, no one wears a leather jacket. It was quite a shock. In the Cariboo, I'm used to seeing my cows alive, walking in long columns through the first driving snow, back to the ranch yards as the crows huddle in the leafless aspens and big trucks spit up huge, white clouds on the roads, or in the spring, as eagles swoop low over the herds in the last gritty, melted and refrozen snow, then take off low over the cars and semi-trailers on the highway. Behind the eagles, the afterbirth streams like ribbons. They land on the last ice by the lake and tear at the placentas with their hooked yellow beaks. The snow melts on the cows' ruddy red backs and rises in thin clouds of steam.

That's what I'm used to.

Toronto might be my brother's town, but what he used to do there, or what he does now in Cincinnati, I'll never know. "It's corporate secrecy," he said when I asked. "This James Bond stuff is real. Except it isn't going on between countries anymore. It's going on between corporations. That's where the real money is to be made."

"I don't think any of them have been to 100 Mile," I said, slowly. I dropped my voice. "I don't think they know where it is."

He didn't get the joke. "They are everywhere. I wish I could tell you. It's to protect you. All I can tell you is I was working in catamenials."

"Ah yes," I said. "Of course." Well, I said it, but actually I felt kind of stupid: I didn't know what catamenials were. But this was my big brother: I wasn't going to let on. So I hung up the phone and opened my eight-inch-thick Webster's Dictionary, the one my mother gave me in despair, biting her tongue, after I said I wasn't going to follow a career in entomology after all and work as a horticultural fieldman for a Washington packinghouse, but was going to be a writer. Catamenial wasn't there. But catamenic was: *monthly, as in the phases of the moon.*

You know, it's great. "You've never seen a more redneck culture on the earth than you see at P&G," Roland told me once. "The language on the shop floor isn't pretty." And think of it: all these redneck engineers aren't going to sit around on the plane, in business class, in front of the pretty flight attendants, and say, "Ya, I'm into tampons. Design 'em. Make 'em. Ship 'em," and sip the whiskey from between the ice cubes in their glasses, or tip their beer back, with their laptop computers scrolling out on their laps. It just won't be done. But it's easy to say, "I'm in catamenials." "Oh yes," the banker says in the next seat, "a good line," all the time thinking, "Boy, I must be dumb or what; catamenials, what in the hell is that?" "A great future!" he says. "Cheers!" Glasses clink.

Go ethnic," Roland said. Hell, that wasn't much help. Everybody was ethnic. After all, I've been in Vancouver. I've heard Vietnamese waiters speaking in heavily accented English. I've heard a Vietnamese waiter in a Möwenpick ice-cream restaurant by the old Roman walls in Zürich, too: the German sounded the same as that Vancouver English! And you know, that made me really happy. It made me feel like we were family. I wanted to give the guy a hug. Still, the bottom line is I go to Zürich every five years. I go to Vancouver once a year. I live in the Cariboo, six hours north of the Coast. I don't think Vancouver is downtown.

Here in the mountain fastness of British Columbia, where the sky lies on the land like the lid on an old blue enamel pot, with the white blotches on it like stars, we were ethnic – once: the Thompson Valley is lined with Salish graveyards and abandoned village sites. From the same era, the goldrush graveyard at Barkerville is full of graves of young men from Italy and France and Germany and New England. They were very young, and they came a long way to die – the oldest man buried there died at thirty-one. But that was a long time ago. Those years of whores and Chinese labour and whiskey and frostbite and gold dust were followed by a century of silence, of ranching in the sun and the snow, of watching eagles curl above black trees like pieces of soot high above a slash fire. Now, after that century, we are stepping at last into modern times. After a long sleep, we are waking up among wild rose bushes and lakes rippling with trout, and we find that we are at the same time three worlds. First, we are the past, telling the modern electronic world about haying; calving; wolves slipping out of the trees and methodically taking first the dogs and then the yearlings; stoneflies, two inches long, rising from the lakes into the sun; moose wintering down in the haystacks and eating a ton of hay a month – each – and knocking down all the fences; horses staring at their reflections in barn windows for the entire day, for company, until you go out in midafternoon and lead them away out of pity: vital rituals. Second, we present an alternative to urban civilization. We have, after all, risen from the same roots but find ourselves now in different relationships to the earth. Both are modern. Both have come through war and technology and love and terror. Third, we are silent, drifting in the starlight: we have as yet found no ways to speak in the world that carry spiritual weight equal to the economic weight of the cities. Money is power. We unconsciously long for that power. And as a consequence of our unconsciousness, we are teaching the young everything out of books. "Run!" we should tell them. "Run as far as you can! We are cheating you!" I did not learn to graft apple trees out of a book, but I have taught men and women to do this work, bent over in long rows of tiny trees, fitting the cambium layers precisely together in the forty-degree sun, as the marsh smells of Osoyoos Lake and Okanagan Lake and Skaha Lake rose up into those hot hills, carrying with them the laughter of tourists and the roar of their Mercury outboards. The smell of the lakes, the contrast between cultures, or even any kind of instruction on how to do that good work, is not in *any* book. We should tell kids that. Work has real rewards. Doing your work yourself has real rewards. In the face of centralized power, that does, of course, make you a peasant. Dismissed.

The next thing I want to hear about you," said Bill Valgardson to me once, "is that you're living with a bike gang, somewhere on the road in Northern Saskatchewan." I never did that, but I did raise twenty thousand peach trees from leafy softwood cuttings in a greenhouse out along the old Great Northern Right of Way south of Hedley, in a town where John Keats is a modern poet. I guess that counts.

One day a man stopped in off the highway to sell me greenhouse plastic. He was travelling through. He walked into the farmyard with his clipboard and his tiny squares of samples threaded on a metal ring, just as I walked back from the chopping block with six bloody chickens hanging from my hands.

"Hi," I said. I smiled. "Just a sec." I dropped the chickens one at a time in the copper boiler on the hot plate and pushed them under the water with a thin cedar board. My wife's entire family was there. We all wore long green aprons sprinkled with feathers and spots of blood. Some families get together every year for a barbecue on the beach and a sing-along around a campfire and volleyball and sunburns. Ha!

Once I had pulled the chickens from the pot and laid them out on the table for my wife to pluck, their feathers grey and matted, I went back out into the gravel and the early morning sun, wiped my hand off on my apron, and shook the salesman's hand. I was young then, and not very experienced at the niceties of doing business. He had a look on his face of complete horror.

The salesman showed me his samples. There was a squawk and screaming from the chicken house beside us. My father-in-law, Corky, walked past, a chicken tucked under one arm, its head poking out, staring inquisitively forward. Two other chickens hung from his hands, their heads curling up just a few inches above ground level, peering ahead to see where they were going. Corky said hello in his thickly accented, fuzzy Danish-English, then cracked a joke: "I'd shake your hand ... but ... my hands are full!" He gave his big, disarming grin. The salesman laughed, but he hadn't understood a word. You could see it in his eyes.

The salesman and I did a few calculations. Wow, his plastic was expensive! I could get it trucked up from Burnaby, right over the Hope-Princeton Highway, for a lot less – and I eventually did. Corky walked back from the chopping block with three dead chickens, the blood still dripping from their necks. He carried them past us, leaving a thin trail of blood in the dust and gravel, then dumped them into the pot. "Watch these, would you, Harold," he said, and stepped back into the chicken house.

"Excuse me," I said to the salesman.

"Don't mind me," he said. "I understand. You're busy." I went into the cool of the shed and poked the chickens down into the hot water to scald them. When I glanced out the doorway, the salesman had gone.

His business card lay there in the middle of the wireweed of the driveway, under a rock.

You don't learn about that in a book.

The question is, if we're not writing about this life and its conversations, what kind of books are we writing?

At the old Eaton mansion in King City, a young man, a third-year literature student, knew what kind of books we have been writing. He hunched down in his chair and asked, "Have you read Rousseau?"

"No, I haven't," I answered.

"Well, you keep talking about land and about getting into the land. So I thought you must have read Rousseau."

"Those things are really important to me, but I haven't read Rousseau."

"Boy, that's so Canadian." He shook his head. It didn't sound like a compliment. "To talk about the land, and to orient yourself to it, to try to get inside it. Whatever that means."

I shrugged.

It's not just Canadian. Even the Norwegians had those dreams. They came to British Columbia in 1909 and settled every available scrap of bad land in mountain valleys. Awash in those dreams, they preferred to settle in the most hopeless land, away from everyone, land that would give them the greatest challenge and the greatest independence – it was less farming than a conversation with God. My grandfather bought one of those abandoned farms below the Evelyn Glacier on Hudson Bay Mountain in 1949: too tough even for the Norwegians. It nearly killed him. But what a conversation!

Today I've cut and split the pine tree that towered above my shed: it was rotten most of the way through and full of long, hollow chambers twelve inches long, with paper-thin walls. In those chambers, lined up side by side, tight together, lay hundreds of ants, one inch long, with long wings the colour of brown sugar: big black ants with strong jaws and mouths twice the width of their heads. Slow and groggy, waiting for winter and a long sleep, they shook out of the wood every time the axe splashed through it. As the ants dropped out of their tunnels, the first snow, half rain, half sleet, fell lightly over my shoulders. It was a few hours of perfectly focussed attention, riveted to wood and the resin sparking through the air as I brought the axe down into the heavy butts. What I affirmed there of the land – that entrance into the land – had a lot more to do with poetry and with modes of attention – programming languages and software applications – than it did with Rousseau. Through the work of our hands we keep the earth alive. The earth, that language of wood and snow, is found in no other way. That whole space where we are conscious, that feeling we get when the wind spills cool through green firs under a bluejay sky, or the long hours as we smell the leather of our gloves while we pitch hay out into the sodden snow for our cattle, is too vast to be contained. The smell of snow slowly rises above the blue diesel smoke and the tang of the hydraulic oil on the air until it swallows us. It is that part of who we are that makes us ourselves.

As I write this in the late afternoon under a sky the colour of sparrow down, an eagle is sitting on the top of a dead aspen, watching out over the last open stretch of water. The ice is white with new snow. The water is deeply coloured, green and purple, swallowing light. There's not a single goldeneye or coot on the water, although yesterday when the whole bay was open there were a hundred of them, swimming in circles to keep the water from freezing around their feet. The eagle is waiting. I think he is waiting for a stupid duck. Poor bugger. He ate all of *them* a week ago. Natural selection is real tough. A week ago I found black and white goldeneye feathers on the lake trail. When I was canoeing through the reedbeds, the eagle shot over my head, very low and very fast, and the goldeneyes curled up off the water in a long arc. Not now. As the first tungsten stars burn through the bromide air the eagle flies off into the darkness of the forest. Hungry.

5

BORDER

TOWN

The day after Heather and I searched for red trees, Maria and I drove north to look for them. She figured this would be a better strategy. As we drove, suburbs flashed past us – an electronic message arcing from synapse to synapse as we passed through the grid. Power lines howled their silence a hundred feet overhead. I was inside that old Apple IIE. Apartment buildings and shopping districts rose up like Mayan step pyramids from abandoned farmland that had grown into weeds, and then sank down. Through the fabric, in a geometrically increasing mass on the low hilltops, writhed old groves of maples: all green. There was not one red leaf to be seen. In the midst of one vast field graded smooth into gravel and sand, the topsoil all buried, barely able to support a little thin, dried grass, one huge, old oak spread its limbs wide and towered high in the blue sky, dark with its leather leaves. It stood there in that farmland that had become too valuable to be farmed and not valuable enough to be built upon, alone, as if abandoned by a civilization that had climbed into its spaceships and left for a distant star. Its leaves were green, too, but a deep green, like a bow drawn across the lowest note of a cello, a sob in the bottom of the lungs.

You can escape the city by air. Maybe. It is impossible to escape the city by car. It covers the whole country with its web. It is where all your dreams come true. It's true: I was happy there as we drove. The whole trip north, the whole challenge to leave the city of dreams, like a climber on K2 with his oxygen tank and the icicles frozen to his beard, was a planetary vision: here was a truly postmodern city. I knew the old, cramped industrial cities of Europe. This wasn't that. This was something else again: its vision was not industrial, but electronic. It wasn't anchored to the earth. It flashed among the stars. For a moment as we drove, I saw the city growing around me, so vast in size that it covered the entire planet and all human activity had become integrated in its web. And I understood why that poet at my reading had turned to science fiction: he was a realist.

As we tried to drive out of the city, we saw mountains on the horizon. As we drove in among them, from one a foul, dumpster wind flashed in through the floor vents and filled the car. Gulls rose in ragged clouds above the summit, like ashes over slow, mouldering fires struck by rain. The mountain was grey, and flat. Huge yellow trucks ground slowly across the summit with their compacted loads. We could have been on the moon.

The next mountain was scentless – sharp and craggy, built of concrete pumped over a wire cage. Trains sped out of tunnels and roared down steep slopes until the mountain swallowed them again whole. It was a profound virtual reality experience: the ghost in the machine, the ultimate core of the grid, that point where the network of the clicking synapses of the city had become so complex it took on a new life of its own. There was no more earth: there on the edges the city curled up in a vast Möbius strip – instead of interfacing with the earth at its borders, it interfaced with itself instead. The weedy trees we had passed earlier were in effect all the earth there is: a wasteland, a garden, a memory, of what no one remembered any more; hence it seemed wild, and strange – like a cancer.

We drove out of the land of mountains. Beside us, men with yellow trucks were hauling dirt around to build a new freeway, like boys in a sandbox with their Tonka trucks and loaders. It was like the time I spent a night in Omak, Washington. The streets were lined with big 4x4s with chrome rollbars mounted with lights. As I watched the men climb down from their trucks and saunter into the cafes and the pizza joint, I could hardly believe it: I had previously seen these images in Hollywood B movies, and had groaned at the caricatures of posses and lynch mobs driving around in trucks like that – cowboys on metal horses. As I sat at the black window of a restaurant in Omak that night, I realized that it might be a cartoon image to me, but there it was reality. In Toronto, too: the freeway sliced for miles through sandy soil, under green and muddy yellow trees, then ended abruptly right at the spreading, white front steps of a Sikh temple. There, directly in the path of the as-yet-uncompleted freeway, the golden onion dome glinted above a close-cut green lawn. I turned in my seat and stared at it behind us for a long time as we drove, as it receded farther and farther behind the tall scrubby grass on the banks of the road.

We left the temple to its geographic brinkmanship and began to drive through those first engines of the delivery of rural land into the urban grid: mansions, with white fences, horse pastures, and fifty-foot pillars above the front doors. Neither city nor country, walled, they were so full of power they had completely cut themselves loose from the grid. They could survive on their own, the electronic echo of a future grid building itself out of the complex nodes of the city. After all, just as there is in language, there are places in the city where power has become so concentrated its interactions have their own life, and just as the city was built on the land, those nodes are built on the city. In the same way, this even-newer colonizing grid was built upon those nodes, tense, vibrating with energy, and no longer in any way recognizably human, on soil no longer recognizably the earth.

It's exactly like the bankers in Tokyo who bought Van Gogh's burning orange and yellow sunflowers for US$45 million and promptly locked them in a bank vault. They lie there in the dark: the painting, like the earth, is something so valuable, so poisonous, so charged with an unpredictable, radioactive power, and capable of spawning such uncontrollable mutagens, that it had to be removed from circulation and hidden in the one place where it could not be seen, in the darkest dungeon of the opposing power in the world, the point of isolation and obsession where we become our enemies and gnaw at them. This is Mozart's opera, *The Magic Flute*! Look out! The Queen of the Night is coming!

As we drove along there in the border district where all of time comes together and fights to become part of the grid, farms unwound past us, with vast, gravel parking lots, pumpkin piles, and petting barns, and then lay there, open behind us like a coffee-table book left out for guests: *A Century of Nude Photography*, or maybe *A Secular Grace: The Barns of Canada*. We were driving through the pages of *Harrowsmith*.

Urban farms. I cranked my head around and stared in wonder as they receded behind us.

I know about border districts. After all, I lived for thirty years in Keremeos, population 850, fifteen miles north of the 49th parallel, with tumbleweeds blowing down Main Street. Obscure clauses in international trade agreements, government bond ratings set by investment firms in New York, all those hieratic texts, those coded urban strings, came down to earth there. In that town, the Columbia Water Treaty between BC and Washington in the sixties, which traded electricity for water and money, didn't have anything to do with low hydro rates, industrial capacity, and government cash flow. It had to do with the irrigation of two million acres of fruitland on the old volcanic basin of the Washington interior, the barren moonscape that inspired Frank Herbert's *Dune* and which against all odds Chief Joseph and the Nez Percé held against the US Army for a decade. The Columbia Basin is a land of greasewood, black stone, and deep coulees with walls of crumbling basalt columns – three-foot-thick black hexagonal crystals stained red and yellow with iron oxides and lichen that have followed the trickles of spring meltwater down the rock for ten thousand years. It is a lean, richly coloured, dramatic, barren country of clear blue skies, and with Canadian water it now bears fruit: one hundred and twenty million packed bushel boxes of apples a year. We can't easily compete against that. In my hometown, our perspective was honed, and clear.

That's what borders are all about: you see things in transition, things which are otherwise hidden. When I lived on that border I lived intimately within the cross-fertilization of US and Canadian farming communities. I drove across the border to buy PVC irrigation pipe, made in Langley, BC, for twenty-five percent less than I could in Osoyoos, on our side of the line. I helped farmers propagate smuggled fruit trees to get around crippling import restrictions. And I lived in the dreams of the Empire. I walked among the uprooted roots and stumps of the first pear trees planted in BC, at the old Inglewood Ranch in Keremeos – trees packed up from Oregon by packhorse in 1898. I walked on the island garden in Keremeos Creek. The old latticework gazebo was already collapsed, but the yellow Victorian climbing roses were still there, twined throughout the red osier dogwoods and the wild clematis and the cottonwoods, the old petals an inch thick on the ground beneath them. In short, I have lived at the edge of the earth, where men and women came from western civilization, from Canada, the US, and from Europe, and where they explored the interface between the earth and the concepts and technologies of civilization, including its philosophers – Rousseau, Keats, Marx, Henry Ford. I know what it's like to live within a border. I know the taste of ozone and the smell of fall water and the cold steel of an engine block in January when the cherry twigs snap at the slightest touch, tubes of ice tinkling like little crystal bells in the still air. In the Möbius strip of North Toronto, I was confronted with its exact urban counterpart. Both in the city and in myself I liked and did not like what I saw. I was swept up by the energy of the city, its vision, and its ability to grant that vision a concrete shape, but its negative shadow, that followed it everywhere, scared me, for although the city had intensified the act of creation, it had intensified its corollary destruction as well. What farms were left were not farms. They were big suburban lots. What Thanksgiving there was, was a postcard view, a factory-grown turkey, a pumpkin sold cheap as a loss leader at Loblaw's. What farmer there was left in myself had become a poet.

The next day, I did not look for red trees: I bought a bag of Golden Russet apples. All my life, I had dreamed of Russets: that apple that grew soft and punky in the heat of the BC desert, nearly ruining the agricultural dream, yet which in the humidity of Ontario grew small and hard and tough – and sweet. I must have peeked into thirty grocers in Toronto, full of Red Romes and Mutsus and Red McIntoshes, all shiny, commercial, tasteless apples. In the last shop there was one tiny box of Russets, for three dollars a pound – antique apples; non-commercial: difficult to grow in volume, not to everybody's taste, not juicy, not pretty. To tell the truth, they looked like potatoes and had a texture like wood. I cherished them. I gnawed at them for a week. I ate the last one in Calgary on my way home, pulling it out of my pocket in the airport waiting lounge, as children ran around me and, despite his obvious confusion, an old man was repeatedly told, "Sir, go sit down. Your flight isn't leaving yet. Sir, you can't go through here. Sit down," and was sternly pushed back and down into a seat.

MARKHAM COUNTY APPLE FAIR, I read on a little white sign stuck into the grass on the shoulder of the road, as I drove Maria's car. I got there, but I was a whole week early. With time to kill, I wandered around, and there, at the Markham Museum, in the border district, I read that urbanization is a natural result of the increasing opportunities for transportation injected into a rural past – which was, after all, only rural out of necessity. Necessity? The fruit farmers of the desert of the Okanagan Valley, dependent on water, were told that same year, along with suburban and urban households, to turn off their irrigation on September 15 because water was short. That the farmers had reduced their water usage by fifty percent in the previous two decades, that they were here first and depended on water for one of BC's largest industries and the backbone of the gentrified English and Californian lifestyle of the Okanagan, did not count, nor did it count that they needed water for one week at the end of October to soak the soil and keep the frost out in the nearly snowless Okanagan winter. The date was arbitrary: September 15. In the end the orchardists petitioned the government in Victoria and got their water. How long will they be able to do that? How long before they are seen exclusively as the past?

Mind you, the people of the city are not totally cut off from the earth. They can see the red trees. They don't need the translation filter of farming life to see them through.

"The trees turn a brilliant red," Maria said, at the wheel, that day we drove north. "It seems as if they are on fire. When you have a tree like that in your yard, your whole house glows with colour, as if the sun is shining inside it. It's very bright. But you never know if a tree is going to turn red. Sometimes it's only one branch that turns colour. All the rest of the tree stays green. Two trees can even grow in the same soil, side by side: one can turn red and the other won't. It's a mystery."

"You need frost," she added five minutes later.

And five minutes later again: "I think it has something to do with the amount of light in the air."

"Look, we're out of the city," she said. She laughed. We were driving more quickly by then, on narrow highways without shoulders. Around us lay abandoned farmland and small country towns, with the wealth that indicates they are not country towns any more, but outposts of the city of dreams. The city whose industry is the contemplation, manipulation, and marketing of images, is colonizing the land with images of the land.

In Kleinburg, Bogart's Yogart was open, under the yellow and green maples. Gift shops and antique shops lined the town's one street. One shop had a sign over its pale green door: TOWN CLEANERS: GIFTS.

In Toronto, I met a new image of humanity. Gone was the physical definition of lives bound to the earth. "This is the end," preaches Leonard Cohen. "This is closing time," and "Everybody knows the good guys lost." Gone was the spiritual metaphor: the dialogue between earth and sky, and the struggle to choose between them. Gone was the humanist metaphor, the geneticist at York working to extend human understanding, Freud struggling to define the human self, and the poet Irving Layton celebrating a man and a woman in a bed, with the light streaming in the window, rather than the hate that separates us.

When I looked out the windows of my school in 1968 and marvelled at Anna and the other hippies who had come to town, young men with *long* hair in that town of military crewcuts, women with *long* dresses walking a half mile to the river with a towel over their shoulder and a bar of soap in their hand, I was still being taught that "man" was defined by his capacity for reason. It was still the Enlightenment. Romantic poetry was still to come. Beauty was still to come. Anna was not yet on fire.

6

SMALL TOWNS,

COUNTRY TOWNS,

AND THE END

OF TIME

In the country-cute town of Kleinburg I thought of the last time I had seen Hugh Dendy. On that December day, Hugh leaned back in his overstuffed chair by his fireplace. Above him towered his books – history, poetry, novels, politics, Marxist literary criticism, and one of the country's largest collections of antique horticultural books. As I paged through *The Apples of New York*, two thick volumes with detailed histories and descriptions of a thousand apple varieties, each one with a hand-painted plate – Golden Russet, American Mother, Black Astrakhan, Wolf River, Lady, Victuals and Drink – Hugh took a deep draw on his pipe, then leaned back and blew smoke rings up to the ceiling. "I have to move," he said at last. "I have to move somewhere where I can walk down Main Street in my own town wearing gumboots and dirty jeans and people won't cross the street to avoid me. Don't laugh! They do! It happened to me yesterday. It's humiliating!" He looked at me as if daring me and took another draw on the pipe. His eyes shone.

What an irony. Four years ago a woman on Gzowski – a Toronto woman with a bright and intelligent voice – called Kelowna, with its twenty miles of strip malls and car lots, a lovely little town in the country and the last perfect place to live: it's only now – after she's said that – that Hugh and I remember the years when a migrant worker, an orchard owner, the packinghouse manager, the doctor, the guy who sold you your shoes downtown, all had prestige, dignity, social honour, and cultural belonging. Hugh and I remember well what it is like to live in a small town. We remember what it was like to define our selves, not to be defined – or even dismissed – by others.

Hugh laughed. "A small town is the kind of place where everybody's problems and transgressions are forgiven." The blue heeler was crouched at my feet, panting, eyes raised expectantly upward. Between her paws lay a wet, chewed-on pine cone. We both ignored her. Blue heelers are crazy. Hugh leaned forward, his voice even. "It wouldn't work in a city, but it works in a small town." He paused. "Until people start to move in. Then it doesn't work anymore. It's no longer family. When it works, it works because everybody knows everybody else. You don't need social workers. Everything is OK. You might have a lot of problems, but they never come to anything. The support and acceptance are there." The dog was whining by then. She pawed at the pine cone a few times, turning it over on the carpet. "Poor old Flinny," said Hugh, and took a deep draw on his pipe.

I worked for Hugh one year. Late one October day after picking apples I found an apple tree in a ditch beside Benvoulin Road in Kelowna. The tree was fifteen years old, rising out of a tangle of overgrown wild roses. In the brambles was a carpet of yellow windfalls. Wasps were feeding on them, clustering, golden, around puncture holes in the skins. The apples were marvelously distorted, the flesh of each one cut by five deep lines, paralleling the five sections of the ovary. Never had I tasted an apple like that! I claimed a couple from the wasps and slipped them into my pocket. With cars swishing past me, I clambered excitedly through a break in the brambles, over a rusted barbed wire fence, and into the field behind. There were two more old trees. One was broken down, overgrown with wild plums and the long, trailing vines of wild clematis. Its apples were shrivelled red husks. The other tree stood alone, surrounded by a thorny ring of her seedling daughters. As I walked towards her, a horse looked up at the far end of the field, then started walking, then running, towards me. We reached the tree together. There were still a few apples in this tree. I picked up an old ten-foot-long prop that was lying in the grass – once used to support branches heavy with fruit – and knocked an apple off. Before I could get to it, the horse had bent down and was eating it. Horses are big. I kept my distance. I knocked another apple off, and another, and another. In the end, of all the apples on the tree the horse ate half and I kept the other half in my pocket. It seemed a fair trade. The horse pushed roughly against my pockets as I left the field. As I climbed over the fence and then up onto the shoulder of the road, she whinnied softly. In the darkness, I walked back down the road to my car. The cars that swished by me sounded like huge animals, roaring.

That night, as the room licked golden and orange in the firelight, we sat on chairs in front of Hugh's fire. Hugh lit his pipe with a long sliver of wood he pulled from the flames, lifting it slowly to his mouth and drawing it in. His father slit each apple open from blossom end to stem end with a planter's knife. As we bit into the apples, six different flavours burst on the tongue, slowly, one after the other, in a slow wash bursting farther and farther back in the mouth and cresting up over the palate like spray from a wave, until the whole mouth was as tender as a blossom.

"This is a great apple," said Hugh, after biting into one of the apples the wasps had been eating in the ditch. "Maybe it's related to Maiden's Blush. There used to be apples in that whole area down there in the Benvoulin. And pears. It was the best pear land on earth. Once. Pear land makes good shopping mall land, too. They brought a lot of old apples here and tried them. Everyone almost went bust at first."

The next morning snow lay two inches deep over the ground. I drove down to Benvoulin Road, cut some grafting wood off the tree, and buried it behind my cabin. The next spring the highways department cleared the ditch. The tree was gone. I got there just in time. I've kept that wet walk beside the dark road in the rain, the cars pouring past me like salmon fighting up a spawning river, driven, and the feel of the apples in my pocket: the golden apples of the Hesperides, the apple that Paris gave to Helen when the three goddesses lined up and said, "Who is the most beautiful?" and he chose.

Over the years, I grafted those apples and spread them around. I gave a tree to Wayne. It's the tree he goes to over and over as he is out in the orchard in the fall – the one he chooses to eat from as he walks through his rows, the pheasants stalking through the grass a hundred yards away. Everyone else is raising or developing apples to sell, giving away the best of their production.

After I rescued the apples from the tree in the ditch, it snowed in earnest. The roads were impassable. At noon, Hugh brought out a bottle of his apple wine from the basement, cooked it on the stove with cinnamon and orange peel, nutmeg and cloves, and poured it into our mugs as the sun cleared away the clouds. As we clustered around the windows, the whole orchard sprang up, glistening like crystal, so white on each cut face of the snow that we were looking directly into the sun.

There is a kind of glow within the physical objects of this world, which is the legacy of the colonial world. As the orchards fall around Hugh one by one, under pressure from the retirement houses of Rutland and Okanagan Mission, he sits in his olive-green house high on the hill above Mission Creek, looking out over the Belgo – The Belgian Orchard Company – why *did* you think we had World War I? – while the trees rise up all around him on the benches, like women brushing out their hair.

There is a watercolour on Hugh's dining room wall: a river among trees, so painted that the water, so clearly the strokes of a brush over matte paper, is actually water. It faces the windows looking west over the orchard and the bench of orchards stretching for miles down to Okanagan Lake. The lake is blue, a pool of light. It is a gap in the earth, through which the sky itself shines. Like the lake, the painting is given depth by water. It is a magical representation, acting as a laser, projecting a hologram around us all, as does the orchard – its context in time – in a parallel but larger sense.

In that painting, and in the orchard, one by one the colours glow, in the exact mathematical relationship of the notes on a chromatic scale of music. That was called Beauty once – the tuning of the landscape. It made no difference whether we called it landscape art or the land on which we walked and in which we worked: it was all the physical shape of a specific relationship between art, land, and life. In short, it was a specific consciousness. Hugh's painting faced the window, through which shone the top yellow leaves of the cherry trees, black with aphids. The trees up against the hand-oiled wood of the windowframe slipped in and out of the picture, just as the water did in the painting facing it.

In the art of Beauty, the art of Victorian landscape, the journey exists for the journey and not to any end. It is a Victorian stroll, with parasols, through the flower gardens of Inglewood in 1898. It is also a boy in 1971 staring down through the boards of the old stage bridge into the cool green water of Keremeos Creek, behind the smithy, and watching the giant trout lurking under the undercut bridge foundations, and going silent, and the digging of the hands into the soil in East Kelowna in 1981, and the smell of the earth on the fingers. Beauty as an organizational concept exists for no other purpose, just as the painting on Hugh's wall exists for no other purpose than this pleasure, this harmony, the binding of all of time into a vision that we can enter, and move through. The ancient artists of memory could build a city in their minds like that, populate it with exotic beings, men whose heads were fire, women who held their heads out before them by the hair, swinging them, women whose breasts were flowers. Then they could return and walk through those buildings and remember, through those images, the world. It was all done for the sheer power of a bear plunging dark-muscled through the glowing fish-blue of a river, a stream of light between scalding banks of stones, the joy of the water cresting before the muscles of the shoulder, and it was an art form that enabled that type of perception.

We had World War I because of that vision – its predominance meant it could be manipulated by people who did not care about it at all. We took things for granted then.

My country, the Interior, and its culture were founded, largely, in 1909, in an era of art, formality, dance, and classicism. It was a time of Beauty and Empire, of honour, loyalty, royalty, polo, snobbism, suppression of Indians, repression of women, and a belief in progress, pianos, and war. Whatever prejudices we bring to this matrix, and whatever knowledge we have gained, whatever we have suffered and endured because of it – however we have grown beyond it – it is still only through that point that we live, however it may have changed in its contact with the wild, inhuman land. We live here at the edge of the wilderness, the edge of the human. We live in landscape. This is the painting entered, and lived. We are the explorers of the terrain of Beauty – strange romantic journey! – just as Fraser and Mackenzie explored the rivers of the West. It is only through that point in time that we enter the past, the stream of history. I've studied German, I've read history, I've travelled to Europe, yet when I walked into the cathedrals of Alsace and Breisgau and Cologne I walked into them through the land, because of the art of that time, the watercolours of 1909, the painting on Hugh's wall.

This art form contains everything of its time, from the spirit writing of W.B. Yeats in 1919, to the work of leaving London, buying an orchard from the Belgian Orchard Company, sailing across the ocean to Halifax, boarding a train, travelling to British Columbia, and coming down from Kamloops to Kelowna, above the blue and burning lake, in the smell of sage and pine, as the meadowlarks call from the trees. Once the image has been made by joining the body and the mind, it takes on a life of its own. Sometimes it is whole, like the last ponderosa pines thundering out of the ravines of Naramata – vertical rivers. Sometimes it is mangled, like a soldier returning from World War I with gassed-out lungs, or no leg, or his mind shattered, or like the orchard community of Walhachin, high above the Thompson River, to which none of the patriotic men returned, and which glows only as a promise and a few wild trees in the sagebrush, and a dark flume snaking along scorched hills.

The night sky above Hugh's glows yellow with the lights of the subdivisions that have in the last two decades pushed through the ravines around him. The grass under his cherry trees glows, pale. There are no stars: no real light. It's like farming in a parking lot.

"I'm almost completely surrounded now," Hugh says. "There's a guy in Nova Scotia who's started a society to fight against streetlights. He says they're unnecessary, they do nothing to combat crime, and they're ugly. I like that. I sent him ten bucks. It might be the best investment I ever made!"

Kleinburg doesn't look like a small town to me. What I know about small towns is they're the kind of place where you say, "God, I hate this place, it sucks, I've got to get out." When people say that, you know you've found the real thing. People in a small town don't know what they have. When you hear instead, "It's so beautiful here," you know you've entered the city. There is no way to escape the city. It goes on forever.

There is beauty in small towns. The people who live in them aren't stunted: they see it well enough. But it is ephemeral. Small town beauty is something glimpsed quickly in passing. In a small town, people live inside the earth. A wind out of the kitchen window – a snowy peak or a high meadow of alpine flowers – fills the house. The colours ripple over your face. You learn not to see the junked cars lying on their backs out in the sagebrush, their brake drums rusted in the rain, as the wind lazes over their broken seats. That's not real life. That's just something you buy. It was never real. You learn to laugh about the burnt-down houses, the charcoal frames still standing, and the blackened, burnt fridges, with the knapweed growing up around them, between the shards of broken glass and the charred, melted aluminum. That's nothing, but the stars above the poplars in late October have great meaning. They place the town in space and time and in the cycle of the seasons. Unfortunately, though, this kind of wealth has nothing to do with public power – it cannot be sold, and nothing can be made of it. It is private. But the mountains are there. They are images. Just like the "country" images of the land in Toronto, they work on us subconsciously. We live within them.

When I lived in the Similkameen I would walk out at night in the dark valley. Along the river the cottonwoods would roar in the dark wind. The wind was so strong that when I breathed I would have to gulp down the air as it streamed over me, yet when I looked up, Nut, the ancient sky goddess of the Egyptians, arched above me, her belly studded with stars. I would stare up from the brown, dusty, windswept valley floor as the wind streamed down from Starvation Flats, fast, like cool molten glass – simply a continuation of the river in the same way the river flows underground, dark and cold, through a thousand feet of gravel below the surface water.

When I left high school in 1975, most of my classmates and I dreamed of going to live in the bush, alone with the world: for some of us it was a log cabin and self-sufficiency, surrounded by snow; for others it was a commune in the cedars of Vancouver Island; for yet others it was to farm in the Nicola or the Peace. Few of us made it. Few of us needed to. All we needed to do was to stand absolutely still. We didn't. We moved to the cities, easily, because we saw ourselves as the city, and we saw our rural culture achieve full expression in the cities. We were taught to see that way. A lot of money was spent on that – endless hours in classrooms learning calculus and stereoscope geography and the history of Cabot and Champlain. And it worked. It worked a lot better on us than it did on the natives in their residential schools. Look at Toronto now. Look at all the subdivisions surrounding Vancouver – vast solar panels unfolded in the interstellar night.

The land is still here, mind you. The conversation has not come to an end. I have walked through the backyards of Hedley at two in the morning in the middle of December, as the whole town gathered to watch a chimney fire, dark shapes walking (parents with their children, their cheap nylon ski jackets pulled close around them), all of us colourless in the night. It was the first fire of the season, and we had all come to see how Moses, the new fire chief – Anna's youngest son – was getting on, and to cheer him on. The fire truck was just a set of wheels and a hose wrapped around the axle. Moses and the other firemen pulled the cart through town by hand: his pickup wouldn't start that night. He was in a panic. It was like the end of an Olympic hurdle race as the firemen ran on the slushy, half-melted inch of new snow, through the lines of people in their dark coats. The fire reflected on everyone's faces. Everyone was laughing and cheering and shouting advice to Moses over the din.

"Watch out for that roof over there, Mosie!"

"Drag the hoses over here, Mosie!"

Red and orange light flickered over everyone's faces. When the fire was out there was spontaneous applause. Then, children sleeping in their arms, everyone drifted home to bed, smelling of smoke.

Diane and I lived in Hedley for two years when we were first married, from 1982 to 1984. It was the kind of town where dogs roamed the streets at night in packs. It was unsafe to go out after dark. On the way back late from the school one night, Diane was bitten by a shepherd fifty metres from our back door. The light pooled around the mercury street lights as if it was a thick liquid. You could see the wind blow through it. The motel was boarded up. Tumbleweeds had drifted against the doors. The Cape Cod wooden lawn chairs sat out under the locust trees, covered with snow and drifted leaves. The sign in the corner read VACANCY. It was unlit.

From 1898 to 1952, Hedley produced ninety-eight million dollars of gold at $32 an ounce. Now it has nothing but itself: old miners' shacks between high, striated, yellow, white, and orange cliffs. The moon rises above them, ancient. Kids go swimming in the deep water among the concrete pilings where the electric plant once stood in the river. Eagles, with dusty feathers, looking as if they were made out of layered slate shingles, hunt above the shacks on the edge of town. The knapweed has choked out all the bunchgrass. Boys dig up skulls in the graveyard and place them on their windowsills. People know each other and love each other in Hedley, but it is a place, like every town in the Interior, where the laws of the lowland don't apply. As you drive east over the Sterling Creek Bridge towards the slag heaps of Hedley, or north past the salt pans and shallow lakes around 70 Mile into the deep Cariboo, you suddenly realize that lawn ornaments don't mean gnomes sitting on toadstools with little fishing rods, nor flamingos stuck in the turf and little green frogs tucked in by the hydrangeas. A lawn ornament here is an old car turned like a turtle on its back, its rusted belly in the air, and fireweed growing through the smashed windows:

valuable, because you can make anything out of it, if you need to. Of course, no one ever does. It's a lot like collecting books: the Proust I bought twenty years ago and still haven't found the time to read.

In Hedley, it's the same: for years the old tarpapered Catholic church was used as an engine repair shop. The cars were driven between rusted piles of metal and stacked-up firewood, in through the front doors, and up to the altar. The firewood has sat there for years. The bottom layers are rotted away. A skunk has built a nest under there. She comes out at night, leaving a thin trail of perfume and vinegar in the grass and used oil. Hedley's not pretty, but you will not find a stronger sense of community anywhere, although it is a terrible lesson in economics and in what is power and wealth and what is not. The grid does not work in Hedley, but Hedley worked for the grid.

When we lived there, only thirty people had a job.

Seven hundred and fifty people in town.

Every boy in my wife's first Grade 7 class in Hedley has now done time in jail – except one. His parents dragged him out of town when he was twelve and bundled him down over the switchbacks of the Hope-Princeton Highway to Vancouver. The problem is, Hedley just doesn't have any horizons – literally or figuratively. The orange, striated cliffs alongside Hedley rise a kilometre straight up above the town on three sides. What you see of the sun for most of the day in Hedley – and for most of the winter – is a line of incandescent white trees along the ridgelines. In all seasons, the sound of rockslides booms and echoes through town. The houses are closed in, too, running from unpainted and snaking collections of rooms modelled after outhouses, to miners' shacks, to stately Victorian and Edwardian country homes, and every other architectural style of the century, most unpainted, most with yards gone to weeds behind rusting wire fences or hedges of gnarled lilacs. Many of the houses are burnt out. On cold evenings the streets of Hedley run blue with damped-down smoke that stings the eyes.

It was Norm who got his son away. Back then in the early eighties, Norm ran the Hedley General Store. It was a vast, sprawling enterprise with a thick new coat of floor paint – grey – to make it more appealing to buyers – and bare white shelves. A few shelves held scraps of groceries, laid out end-to-end to present a bold front, some of them almost antique. Best-before dates were not of the greatest importance to Norm. A big man, with slick hair and a rumpled white shirt and hanging jowls, a loud voice and at times a happy smile, Norm held court behind his counter, tearing the corners off unsold Vancouver *Province* newspapers so he could claim for them when the new ones were delivered on the morning truck making its run to the Alberta border.

"I told them at the school," says Norm, "to take my son out behind the school and beat him with a pipe if he gave them any lip." Rip! "I'm serious!" Rip! "Look! I told them, I'll sign a piece of paper; make it all perfectly legal!" Rip! "Dave told me he'd love to do that, but he just can't. What bullshit. That's what's wrong with this country." Rip!

The door creaks open, letting in a shaft of light, and then bangs shut, with its PROVINCE SOLD HERE sign glowing like a blue icon in a Russian monastery. Another of the town's retired miners joins us at the counter. From Rossland, Sparwood, Fernie, and Kimberley, when they are finished with the mines they retire to Hedley and live on their pensions of $300 a month. Economic reality has lifted out an entire strand of Canadian culture and concentrated it – like ore in a crushing mill – in Hedley.

"Have you tried to go through the School Liaison Committee?" I ask. "I mean, to get something to change?"

Norm laughs and shakes his head.

"No, I didn't want to get involved. I could see what's going on. So I said, 'You need someone there who doesn't care which way things go – who doesn't have a stake in things.' That's how these things work. And that's not me. It's all just bureaucracy." He laughs again. "It's a good excuse, don't you think?"

I laugh and agree. My heart's not in it, though. I still think talking would help, but Norm's imposing and I'm young and just as speechless in my own way.

A little old lady who has been soaking her hair in Mrs. Williams' Blueing shuffles up to the counter with some arrowroot biscuits and a banana. Norm rings them in on an old manual cash register that should be in a museum, except there is no museum, just this store, all that is left of the bustling city of Hedley – five hotels, two churches, two mines, and a crowded main street, where miners spent a wild night on the town after hitching a wilder, jury-rigged ride on the ore tramlines down the cliffs. One by one the hotels burned down. The last mine closed in 1952, when the ore came out as such a matrix of copper and gold it could only be separated at great cost – greater than the value of the gold itself. Year by year the city became a town, and the town grew farther and farther away from the world.

The cash register dings and the drawer flies open.

"That's the way it is in this town," Norm says, dropping his voice, conspiratorial, as he counts out the change. "Look at this mess last year with the skating rink. The thing was built and then the committee went up and tore it down, because the work hadn't been passed by the committee. They want you to do things on your own. You won't find anyone pulling together. But once you get going on your own, once you do something, once you start, they stop you. You're a threat."

As every day goes by, Norm grows more bitter. He bought this store a decade before, as part of a dream, to get out of the city and into the country, to lead a simpler life.

"We were on a trip," he says one day, after I asked if there had been any nibbles on his store. I had come in for bread, milk, cereal, and one of those *Province* newspapers. "We saw the store and bought it on an impulse. Two weeks later, we were back, and in business. God, were we naive!" he laughs. All the loose flesh on his pale, colourless face shakes. His small dark eyes are steady, however, like pebbles in an alpine stream, soaked with water and sun. "We should have stayed in town for a week and then made up our minds!"

It wasn't just Norm who was going crazy in Hedley that year. The principal of the school, Dave Smith, was losing his mind as well – and at an even greater rate. Like Norm, he tried to cover it up with bravado and good humour; like Norm, he was a big and physically powerful man; and like Norm, his depression often broke through his veneer of joviality. When that happened, he sounded very small and very afraid.

Dave had been an RCMP officer in Princeton, a larger mining and forestry town forty-five minutes up the valley, which had not yet seen its mine collapse. The few men in Hedley who actually had a job worked at the mill in Princeton. Policing, however, was just not Dave's thing. What's more, he was terribly homesick for Newfoundland. Luck shone on him, however, when he fell in love with and married Arlene, the town sweetheart. With three generations behind her in Princeton, her roots were deep.

In 1980, the Hedley school was administered from Princeton and was renowned for violence. When it needed a new principal, Dave was pushed forward – as far as anyone I talked to in Hedley could figure out, to get him set up to take care of Arlene. When the town committee heard that Dave had been an RCMP officer, they were won over immediately. A tough-guy approach was, they figured, just what was needed to straighten the kids out. So it was that Dave and Arlene moved to Hedley, where Dave's unhappiness could really fester.

I sat across from him in his kitchen as he shoved a three-inch-thick stack of paper towards me. Dave was hoping to cash in on the fashion for police novels by writing of his experiences in Princeton. The novel was all very gothic and took place mostly at night and over bottles of whiskey, as a shy young constable fell in love with the town's untouchable belle, at the same time as his job overwhelmed him. The story was set along the river, twenty minutes outside of town, among old farmhouses with a ring of motorcycles parked amid the wrecked cars and snarling dogs on a moonlit night. At the high point of the novel, the point at which this dual life came to a point of decision, or awareness, our hero – we might as well call him Dave – was called out there alone. The door of the car opens and Dave, holding his flashlight in front of him like a club, advances forward into the dark.

He was suspended for shooting one of the dogs.

As we drink Dave's homemade wine – rough stuff that coats the inside of your skull with a sheet of iron and then beats upon it with a ballpeen hammer – I try to explain to him about the rudiments of plot and character, showing him the structure off of which he could really hang his story.

"It has been rejected by a lot of publishers," he says. "I really don't know what to do with it now."

But Dave just can't keep his mind to the story, and I'm still young enough to think that for some reason he has to, that he actually wrote the novel as a piece of literature, not as a plea to be heard, not as a way to understand himself or place himself in the world. And so our conversation wanders, with Dave trying to talk about anything but the story, and me searching to bring these threads back and weave them into the novel I spent the previous week reading.

"I took my boy up to see the ballpark," Dave says. "Every summer dozens of ball teams from around BC come to play here, so I thought my boy and I could go up and throw a few balls. A dad has to do things like that with his son. The ballpark was right below the dump, so we went up there, too. I just wanted to spend time with my son. It was terrible, though. Someone had shot a doe out of season and had dumped the guts and its unborn fawn up there. It was July. Can you imagine someone doing that? It's depressing. When my boy asked me what it was, I didn't know what to say about that. Why should I have to explain all about that to my five-year-old son?" Dave's voice rises. "I have to get out of this town." He pours himself another glass of rough wine.

I stare across the table at him. His eyes are scared. I can see at once that he doesn't belong here, that he wants someone to tell him that he doesn't have to be crazy. I know what he means, though. In my first month in Hedley I had already seen kids shitting on their back lawn, the guts of a goat left to lie on another front lawn – where it had been butchered – and kids on the roof of their shack throwing kittens down into the open septic tank in the back yard. I tell Dave about it. Dave's eyes are still dark and afraid.

"You have to roll with the punches," he laughs, trying to shake the weight off, but it will not shake off.

It's no wonder. I already had some personal experience with Dave's troubles. Diane and I were living in the house that had sheltered Dave and Arlene the year before – a small two-bedroom teacherage under an old McIntosh apple tree riddled with coddling moth, every apple weeping with sawdust and wormholes. We liked the house a lot, until the cold weather came and we had to turn on the furnace. White powder, stinking of pesticide, blew out of all the ducts. It was bad enough watching the level of heating oil drop alarmingly quickly in the tank off the back porch. This was worse. Diane was growing sick.

A visit to the secretary-treasurer of the school district soon cleared things up. It seemed that a year earlier, weaver ants had made a spectacular two-foot-high nest under the back porch and were moving into the house. When Arlene had found them marching in long columns across the floors, she had called Dave at work. Dave took care of them. When she found them crawling in swarms over her baby in the crib, she told Dave to fix the problem or she was going back to her parents in Princeton. And so the school board brought in an exterminator, who laid white powder along the bases of all the crawlspace walls. The ants died, but the powder remained – for me. As the teacherage was an old building, it was not airtight, and the powder was being sucked up into the heating system. Another call from the school board, this one on my instigation, brought the young poison men back. They said they couldn't understand how this could happen, "and besides, the stuff was completely harmless." They did vacuum out the furnace ducts and cleaned all the powder from the crawlspace. They declared us fit as a fiddle. It was not to be. The powder still blew. It is sixteen years since we lived in that house, and Diane still suffers from asthma and complete intolerance to any perfumes or scents. I knew what Dave meant, alright.

I saw Dave again a few weeks later, after the open house at the school. After Norm left with his family in a flurry of ebullient cynicism, I checked all the rooms upstairs for Diane, turning on the lights, checking for stragglers in the empty, deskless spaces under the wide walls of windows as the dark poured in from the night. The lights of cars turning the corner on the hill into town from the west swept across the walls, and the red lights of cars – in town for bingo – flared through the old, rippled glass, from the community hall parking lot across the road. I would stand there briefly in each room, it would feel like 1933, then I would turn the lights off again. In that way I walked down through the school, turning on the lights in front of me and turning them off behind. I clumped down the hall, then down the wide stairway, where the black rubber stair runners were worn down by thousands of feet, to the main floor. Down there, the classrooms were still in use. Dave was standing in front of his office, joking with Diane. I told them that the upstairs was clear and then walked down the hall, looking at the posters and artwork that the children had put on the walls for their parents.

I stopped.

The Grade 5 class had done an exercise in imagination: "When I Grow Up."

I called Diane over. She read.

When I grow up I'm going to live somewhere where I can have a bath every day.

"I know," she said. "When I saw that, I almost died."

Norm did manage to sell his store in the end, to a Hindu shopkeeper who had just fled the nationalization of Indian businesses in Fiji. Like Norm before him, he bought the place virtually sight unseen, and while Norm was settling into freedom with his family at the Coast, the new owners were discovering their own kind of Hell. In the familiar pattern, their dreams of freedom collided with the stark realities of Hedley. Within a week, the store had ceased to be the centre of the community. The new owner's heavily accented English and strong sense of propriety – and what was by Hedley standards rudeness – drove nearly everyone away. The owner was a big, pockmarked man who protected his pretty young wife fiercely. If a man came to the till, he would glower over him, daring him to say a word to his wife, while she rang in the items, her eyes cast down. He had absolutely no contact with anyone in town, aside from his sourness behind the till. Sales, which had never been good, plummeted.

Three months after he bought the store, it burned down. The word was that he had just put on extra fire insurance. The family left town that same day. The weeds grew.

Dave wasn't long for town, either. He took the first out-of-town job he could get – back in Princeton, up the valley. His fairy-tale marriage lasted for two more years before Arlene left to become a hairdresser in Penticton.

Dave didn't last long in the valley after that. He bought a private security firm in Penticton.

We stayed in Hedley for another year and then left as well, for Keremeos, thirty minutes south. Behind us all, Hedley remains, slowly falling in upon itself, a little grubbier and more rundown every year. The weeds grow higher in front of the houses. New houses burn down every winter, with nothing left except a few blackened pots and pans set up on posts around the yard like charms on a high trail in Nepal. Hedley is shrinking, fiercely loyal, turned in upon itself, and alone. There may be no economy there at all, but it is the Canada I know – not the hyperculture of media and hype, but slow deep attitudes that rise with the seasons and unshakably change the perceptions.

Two years after we left Hedley, I attended a film series in the Hedley Community Hall. I drove north once a month along the ice floes and silver water of the night river, and through the shining white hayfields of the Indian reserve. It was a touring series of foreign and Canadian art films sent up on the bus by the Pacific Cinematheque, an eclectic film society in Vancouver's West End. In Hedley, the series was hosted by the Hedley Historical Society. The hall was better known for its Thursday night bingos: people would drive a hundred and twenty miles to come to those, with the cigarette smoke descending hour by hour in a nearly impenetrable cloud from the ceiling; by 10 p.m. it would stabilize in a perfect plane a metre off the floor. Old women would carefully set up their good luck charms before them, lay out their fifty cards in perfect order, and with their dabbers and plastic chips wait for the numbers to be called. One old woman with blue hair had a foot-high gold Buddha. Between every number she rubbed its tummy for good luck. Stakes were high: a thousand bucks a game. The Hedley Historical Society was better known for its summer guided tours of the mine tailings, in costume: parasol, lace, long dress, bustle, tough black leather shoes coming halfway up the leg, with fifty tight buttons the size of pearls: TOURS MEET AT THE CENOTAPH AT 1 PM SHARP! BRING A GOOD PAIR OF WALKING SHOES! Posters were put up at the hamburger joint at the Gulf Oil station. Attendance was poor, but never so poor that the tours were cancelled.

On the first night of the film series, there was half a crowd. Moses was there in the parking lot with his old green pickup. Everyone talked together for ten minutes outside, then drifted in. A bitter wind was blowing down off the old mine buildings on the cliff three thousand feet above us in the starlight.

The slush had frozen to a hard black ice that crunched under our feet. The stars were made out of crumpled-up cigarette wrappers.

That was the winter the dump was closed down in Hedley. It used to be a great place to go shopping. If you needed anything, chances were you could find it there in one form or another. The dump used to be full of giant, scavenging ravens. With their six-foot wingspans they would wheel and lumber slowly around you as you emptied out your garbage and replaced it with someone else's, their claws dragging long, mysterious tracks across the snow. It looked like writing. In that setting it was hard to believe that it wasn't. The dump sat up against the scree slope above town. It was closed down because people still insisted, against regulations and despite warnings from the Ministry of Environment, on burning it weekly. The dump had been burned weekly for eighty years. For eighty years of Sundays, the choking, poisonous smoke had settled in all the streets. It would soak into your clothes and under the sashes of your windows. When the dump was finally shut down, all the garbage from the Thursday night bingos at the hall was stacked in big plastic garbage bags in the entrance way. We had to thread our way in through them. It was dark and cramped. I laughed: "Only in Hedley!"

"Don't laugh," said Deb, walking up behind me. She was one of the geologists at the mine, working the Vancouver Stock Exchange in the cliffs and scrub forests and basalt outcrops in the high country across the river. "Anybody who goes to Keremeos takes a load along in their truck." She smiled. "You bring your truck?"

So, after the show that night, I wound back through the obsidian night of the winter valley, with the ice along the river glowing a dull, pale green in the starlight, with a load of cigarette butts and crumpled paper behind me. My hands smelled of ashes.

All winter long, I made the pilgrimage to Hedley. The films were exhilarating, and gave me the world: *I've Heard the Mermaids Singing*, by Patricia Rozema, *The Stationmaster's Wife*, by Fassbinder, and even *Coup de Grace*, by Volker

Schlondorff: black and white, brutal, detailing the conflict between fascists and communists in the Balkans after World War I. Hedley was the perfect setting for that.

We had only one projector, and an old torn screen patched together with strapping tape and rolled up on two long one-and-one-half-inch-thick wooden curtain rods. By the middle of the winter, when it was thirty below and the wind curled in under the door in a thin drift of snow and flowed around our feet, we would each be dressed in three layers of socks, felt-pack boots, longjohns, two layers of pants, two sweaters, down jackets, hats, heavy mitts, and we would still be so cold there in the unheated hall that we would get up while the projectionist was changing reels and run around the hall to warm ourselves, slapping our shoulders with our arms. We would laugh at how silly we must have looked. "Only in Hedley!" Deb or I or even Moses would shout. Someone always brought a dog, a big shepherd-Lab cross, and he would run around with us as well, his nails clattering on the polished wood floor. He'd slip out on most of the corners.

By the end of the series, no one was there but the projectionist and myself. You had to be dedicated to see a film in Hedley. You had to endure a lot. It was like those talent nights they used to have in town. Moses organized those. They would go on for five excruciating hours, because people would keep showing up and asking, "Can I go on, too?" and Moses would slip them on to the end of the list, and all the time young children would play tag and hide-and-seek up and down the aisles and in front of the stage, screaming, with the dogs running with them, barking loudly.

The projectionist sat at the back by the machine, as it whined and clicked through the film. I sat up front by the speaker. Tinny, in a scratched, grey metal case, it sat right on the floor. Ten feet in front of me, a thin grey wire snaked out behind it, then wound back fifty feet along the side of the hall to the projector. All through the film the projectionist and I would call to each other and laugh. Our voices echoed in the big room. I don't think I've ever been so cold, but it didn't matter: even though under those scarred basketball hoops it felt like I was watching films after the fall of civilization and after the end of time, never have I seen such great films. The colours from the screen flickered over our hands and faces. The room smelled of wet wool and thin coffee. It was a ritual of wealth. The series lost $250. That was the end of that.

Moses had the most beautiful building in Hedley, two old storefronts which he had lovingly restored. He had inlaid all the interior walls with strips of cedar, fanning them out along the colours of the grain into conch shells and suns – as if the whole building was a scatter of driftwood on a gravel bar, one of those big drifts that come up in the Similkameen River in flood and snag against the sandbar willows, making wooden fields an acre in size, high above the water line, tangled with a few old fishing floats and tires and rusted aerosol tins. The Golden Nickel Restaurant was the name of the joint, and Moses was very proud of it. When Moses was not fighting fires with his crew, he was hanging out there, cooking in the kitchen, serving his inimitable mushroom salad and his sweet ribs. His friends would stop over for a game of cards. If there were tables to wait on, they would get up from the cards and coffee and help Moses out by taking down your order. After Norm left, it was the centre of town.

One night, however, the good times came to an abrupt end. Some young kids started threatening Moses. After all, he had beautiful silky hair down to his waist; what more temptation could you want? Moses went out to them in the blue Hedley dusk, in front of the spreading glass wall of the Golden Nickel, apparently with a baseball bat in hand. Rumours flew – that his brother John joined him and Moses laid into the kids with the bat, as things got out of hand, and, alternately, that they all yelled at each other for awhile until Moses walked away, to keep himself calm. Don't get me wrong, things can get more than a little out of hand in Hedley, where nerves are raw. It would be understandable behaviour, in a place like Hedley. If Moses had been put up in front of a jury of his peers – a jury of those who lived in Hedley – all charges would have been thrown out of court. Moses was not, however, and so, with allegations against him, allegations which he firmly and convincingly denied, he entered a protracted trial. It transformed him completely. It was as if with every – real or imagined – stroke of the bat on the heads and backs of those boys, they had thrown a stone through another plate glass window of the Golden Nickel, and the glass lay all over the street in long splinters and shards.

The first change was that Moses cut his hair short, went clean-shaven, and gave up his hand-woven clothes in favour of jeans and cotton shirts. He was under the tutelage of a lawyer by this point and was doing everything he could to translate his good name in Hedley into something people elsewhere could recognize as a good name. After three years, the case was still trickling through the courts, but Moses had closed down the Golden Nickel and had moved to Keremeos. There he could hold down a job, distance himself from the night of threats and glass, and shine with a more easily recognizable respectability. The restaurant is still a restaurant in Hedley, and people still drive the four hours from Vancouver to dine there, but Moses doesn't cook there anymore. With Moses's transformation, the old dream which Anna had brought from Toronto ended. That story of social revolution and renewal which had provided the valley with a path out of poverty and isolation had closed. The long-standing and unspoken debate in the cultural fibre of the community, between the urban values of Ontario, which Anna brought to us from so far away, and the values of the valley itself, had turned full circle, like a mink gnawing off its tail in a trap. It was the purest image yet of a valley struggling to define itself in a world which had changed so greatly that it no longer fit into it. After twenty-five years, the gap had become so great that it had to be bridged, and with tools inappropriate to the job, and with disappointing results.

You would think it would be otherwise, given that the mines of Hedley are working again. The old Nickel Plate Mine, four thousand feet up the sheer, buckled, and upthrust cliffs, the long underground stopes opening as small, square, dark holes in the cliff face, with long, grey cones of rubble beneath them, works twenty-four hours a day: an open pit operation. The top of the mountain is slowly being eaten away, like those old myths of the waxing moon being eaten by a dragon. The glow from the yellow sodium lights flares across the night sky, obscuring the stars. There is never any night in Hedley anymore, yet the jobs don't go to Hedley – that might make up for it. The workers are bussed in from Penticton, on the other side of the mountains.

By 1995, the tailings were being reworked, too: grubbed up by a giant blue crane, dumped onto conveyor belts, carried under the highway, and spilled out onto the dry ground by the cemetery. They were heaped up in tall piles, flat on the top, on a sea of blue plastic tarps. Long lines of aluminum irrigation pipes were laid out on them, and the sprinklers sprayed out white in the hot, windy air.

"It's a clever system," said Deb's husband – like her, a geologist across the river. "They tried it out in the laboratory, with really small amounts of material. They never tried it out in any practical sense. It's losing money. The water isn't to keep down the dust. But it does do that. The water and the air react with the cyanide in the tailings to produce acid. The acid binds with the gold. Then it's leached out with the water. The water collects at the bottom, drains out into a settling pond, then is pumped over to the processing building. After that, it's just a simple chemical process to get the gold out. They're getting gold, but it's costing too much. They're not getting enough."

The big trucks brought the tailings from above town, too. For fifty years the tailings sat in long narrow ponds, buttressed by rotten old lumber, along the sides of 20 Mile Creek, slowly eroding away every spring. Only after a big fight did the people of Hedley keep the trucks from driving through the residential streets. Finally, Eldorado, the mining company, agreed to build a new road, on the other bank of the creek. No one wanted that cyanide floating through their yards.

Hedley got nothing from this work either.

The cemetery, there on the side of the now-abandoned settling ponds, is choked with knapweed and tumble mustard. Many of the graves are fallen in, with deep holes snaking black through the collapsed gravel. The barbed wire fence is rusted and half fallen down beside the highway.

Country and the beauties of the country are urban constructs. *Harrowsmith* is an urban magazine. The country has its own images. They have to do with human relationships, not with economic ones. Economic relationships are where we who live on the land are poor. People who live on the land consider themselves to be living at the centre of the world. They are, of course.

It's great, you know. You have to love the ironies. I, who was raised on a farm, went to Kleinburg and saw the country for the first time. There were shops selling crafts and pottery. There were T-shirts, for kids, with TORONTO written out big, and on some even TORONTO CANADA under a picture of five little Indian boys in buckskin jackets, brandishing tomahawks, whooping. There in Kleinburg, in the lunchroom of the McMichael Art Collection, I was happy. I had come home. There it was at last: Canada. That big pink country I had heard about all through my childhood. We studied it. It used to sprawl at the top of the world, on the map with the foot-long Nielson's chocolate bars in the corners, where dragons and sea serpents used to go. It really existed after all. It didn't just roll up above the chalkboard so we could use the board for math class.

One day we had stared at the map as the principal pointed out all the parts in pink. There were a lot of them. He said, "That's the Empire. We're part of that. There was the Roman Empire once, but this is the greatest empire there ever was. This is The Empire on Which the Sun Never Sets!" He was so excited. He went on to draw arrows coming down from China into Vietnam, his long wooden pointer sweeping through the air, and explained why it was necessary for the US government to bomb Cambodia: to keep us free. "Communism is a disease. It has to be stopped. First they will take over Vietnam, then Australia, then us here, in Cawston." The pointer sketched a long arrow across the Pacific. We were in Grade 6. We had never heard of Cambodia, or communism, but what the heck, we watched the news that night with a new appreciation: the long lines of refugees in Vietnam with their bamboo carts and bullocks, and the GIs with their guts in their hands. We had been taken into the know. And Canada was part of that Empire. Wow!

C anada is real. It is not just a valley of wild currants and cottonwood leaves. Actually, it is not that at all. I have seen it now. It is a country of pumpkins in autumn fields, a country of red trees, quaint farms, and brick houses. It's the rustic decor of the McMichael Art Collection dining room: stone walls, wooden beams, carvings of moose and beaver recessed into dark wood panelling. Rustic I already knew, from the Cariboo: log cabins, and chopping blocks out behind the chicken pen, and farmers' pickups full of used twine, tools, and broken pieces of pipe and wire. But not this kind of rustic. Yet it was my own. I recognized it immediately. I had stepped into the schoolbooks of my childhood. I knew every smell, every grain of the wood, every flake of the stone, and despite my shock I was really happy. Anything could happen now. Everything was alright. When I saw Tom Thomson's cabin in the green maple woods at Kleinburg, a huge weight fell off my shoulders, as if I had just eased a huge pack of beaver pelts onto the ground after a two-year journey west to Lac La Hache and the land of the Okinokane and the Nez Percé. For the first time in my life there was no discrepancy between the images of the land and the land itself. All my life I had dreamed of living in this kind of landscape – all of us who have gone farming in British Columbia have dreamed that – but it is one of the truths about the jackpine forests of BC that such landscapes do not exist. We've all had to come to terms with that. What's more, our attempts to translate the land into such images look either pathetic, suburban, or tangled in frustration and despair, with a lawn full of junked logging equipment, ramshackle chicken coops, and rusted loops of cable corroding in the air, caught up in old aspen leaves. But such a country really does exist.

That was one shock. The other was the art. It was as if

Cézanne had gone out for a holiday in the bush and had got himself lost, so lost he'd even forgotten who he was. His mind had vanished. He was the trees. He was the paint. He was half-melted and refrozen snow. He was a biting wind. The McMichael Art Collection holds the work of the Group of Seven. Or I should say: the work of the Group of Seven is there, but in an unusual form. It is not held. These aren't calendar reproductions, after all, picked up off a tall stack at the drugstore in December: the real art of the twentieth century. This is nineteenth-century art. This is art of the years of the wars. In this kind of art, painters confront the landscape and record their impressions. Can you imagine? Thomson and Jackson froze their fingers off out in the bush, laying down the earth in smears and dribbles of paint. It's like the Bohemian waxwings that hang around all year, yet you only see them for two days: once in the late fall as they flit through the aspens for a day, eating soapberries in the first snow; then once again in the spring, when they return to tenderly eat the blossoms off the saskatoons, slowly making their way across the land.

Here in the Interior we have entered the modern world without losing the old world at all. There's no such thing as social evolution here. There is a depth in time. It's like talking to people in Germany and discovering that the ballad and fairy-tale traditions are still alive, as literature, although in English they have been dead for two hundred years. It's something you hang onto tightly. But I have also been to Toronto; I have walked through my own dreams. There is no past in Toronto; there is no present. Tom Thomson's cabin is a door. You can either step out from those clapboard walls into the parking lot or out of the parking lot into the vision held by that small room of dark walls and crystal windows, with the reproduction of a painting set on the easel, or you can make the doorway the vision – you can embrace both possibilities. This is what Thomson did, by exploring the movement of paint on the canvas. The world is under tension, trembling, alive, just on the edge of apprehension. This was Thomson's work. Beneath the arc-flashes and algorithmic codes and pre-stressed concrete containment shells of the dream city of Toronto, this is a Toronto vision, still. Look at it: long groves of sumacs are blasted by frost and curl down through the city on the river; a Huron wind splashes against the glass walls of the CN Tower, as kids sit inside, big virtual reality glasses over their eyes, shooting down spaceships.

In one painting by A.Y. Jackson, all the stars of early dusk are clustered in the centre of the sky, white above trees and water. They look like rips in the canvas. I walked down towards them, between a hundred feet of gold-framed rivers and waterfalls and bruised bromide lakes just before storm, to see what had damaged the painting. As I stepped up close, I saw that the marks were actually not rips at all. They were stars: quick jabs with a dry brush – stars at the moment in the pale blue evening when the sky, although still blue, suddenly turns transparent, and the first stars are there. It is not the look of the stars that is represented there, but the sudden glance of apprehension that drew Jackson's eyes from the trees, out of his peripheral vision, and the stars were there where they were not.

In Tom Thomson's studio (or shack, as they call it there in Kleinburg) the furniture is crammed into the balcony – chairs and tables stacked tightly on top of each other as if they were in the back of a moving van in the bush north of Lake Superior, going west in a blizzard in mid-February. In a clear, white, shadowless light on the studio floor below are a plastic laundry basket full of Crayola felt markers and a dozen plastic chairs. The floor is marked with masking tape and square-edged blotches and sprays of paint: pictures have been taped down there. The studio that used to stand in a ravine in Toronto, frozen in the winter, has become a schoolroom.

The windows are large, made of five-inch-square plates of bevelled glass set in unpainted wooden sashes. Staring through them was exactly like watching my grandfather back in '69 building a sailboat by hand in his workshop in Naramata, with his hand-made lathe and hand-forged chisels. To keep out the cold he slowly filled up the walls with sawdust and shavings as he made them – stud by stud for five years: most of the time his fingers were frozen and blue, and his thumbs were black with huge blood-blisters and burns, with saw marks across his knuckles. There was the low flicker of a woodstove in the corner, and frost thick on the glass: an industrial site. There was nothing pretty about it, except its functionality and its sense of use.

I stood on tiptoe outside Thomson's door, peering into that same stillness. I thought of the girl in the Robert Munsch story who coloured herself from head to toe with Super Indelible Never Come Off Until You Die And Maybe Even Later Colouring Markers: not a good idea! She rectified her mistake by colouring over herself again with normal markers, exactly the colour of her clothes and skin. She did the same with her father. He looked better than ever: bright, and full of life. Even her mother agreed, her lips pursed wistfully. Then it rained. Another bad idea. The normal markers washed off. Dad didn't look so good anymore. Those were the markers alright, in Tom's cabin.

After a day of heavy wind, the temperature in the Cariboo last night dropped to twenty-six below. At midnight the clouds fell: a thin breeze of tiny crystals falling silently through the air and stilling the air as they fell. Today the sky is apricot at the tree line. Above that it is white. Steam rises quickly from every inch of the lake surface. A crescent of ice has formed along the reedbeds; fog drifts in torn ribbons, quickly, east, over the lake surface. The lake is cut up, lightly chopped, but as it moves only one quarter of the speed of the fog, the whole effect is of a shimmering veil. The opposite shore of the lake, where the water is deep, is in heavy shadow. The near lake burns: a pool of brilliant white milk, swirled with streaks of the sky. It is a living creature of light come down today among us, and only the water within the light, that is its carrier, makes it livable for us, but it is livable. After half an hour the light is too bright to look at, but the crescent along the reedbed is the black of the pure night between the stars.

People come a long way to enter the painting in which I live – retired Americans driving in convoy up Highway 97 in the biggest pickups they can buy, pulling fifth-wheel trailers. Their license plates say WYOMING and KANSAS. Their faces are set and serious. Their wives have tightly curled permed hair. Around the tongues of their trailers, the boxes of their pickups are piled high with tarps, ropes, jerry-cans of gasoline, and spare tires. You have to feel so good for these guys: they're off to drive the Alaska Highway. Sure, they drive so slowly and they hug each others' bumpers so close it's pretty hard to pass them, but you can't be angry with them: they have been dreaming of this since they were twenty years old. If in the meantime the Alaska Highway has become a safe, easy road to drive, and Alaska has drifted farther south, so what. It's not often you see someone follow a dream with such enthusiasm.

There beside those retired men and women, the five hundred Black Angus and Hereford cows of the Monical Ranch, brought in from the summer range, graze along the highway like wildebeest on the Serengeti. Across the highway, a cowboy on a dark brown horse, a blue heeler running ahead of him, herds the bulls down, thirty big tanks of semen, like noncoms rushing into the streets of Somalia armed to the teeth, the steroid-fed muscles rippling heavily under their loose skins – helpless, stupid prisoners of their hormones, but filled with strength and a troubled assurance.

While the Americans drive north, I watch the bulls come down to the yard. A few geese skid through the blue air overhead, as white as puffs of condensed silver. I have just burned the last of the summer's grass, walking through pools of blue smoke as heavy as mercury in the lungs. I have come down for the fresh air. The moon is in its first quarter: a thin shell of abalone above the pink clouds and green sky of dusk, floating. It is like the pink rose blossoms of spring.

It is late fall, under pines. The flower stalks are yellow and collapsed into themselves. The aspens are stark and grey. The air smells of snow. Last night the moon was a pan of ice. The clouds drifted across its face like snow over the winter lake, among the clattering reeds; each grain of cloud clung to the moon, replacing a mote of the moonlight, which tore off in its place: the moon was a constantly regenerating stillness, like the grains of sand that form a ripple on the bed of the Shuswap River at Enderby, with the cottonwoods, as deeply wrinkled as elephants, leaning way over the slow current, ancient, in their thundering silence. It smelled like snow, too. I was excited for that clarity, that rest. Snow is a healing.

In the winter, when everyone flies off to Hawaii and Disneyland, and most of my parents' generation hit the road for the world's biggest flea market in the desert outside of Quartzite, Arizona, and to golf in Palm Springs, and to gamble in the riverside casino at Laughlin, I am so happy to be able to get my snow shovel out of the shed and to be able to say, "I'm staying. Right here."

I'm staying. Right here.

This is the centre of the world.

Among the portraits of the Canadian Shield at the McMichael Art Collection, I saw something totally out of place: totem poles painted by Emily Carr. They seemed lost. I've touched those poles, those sad owls, that necklace of skulls, as Carr did, in Kispiox, in the rain. I went there when I was young – as Carr was when she went. In fact, I was so young I had no real voice to speak with yet. I was swimming in a river of images. Mostly I was swept inexorably downstream, sometimes in a broad deep current, sometimes in white water, smashed against rocks and log jams. Carr's totems looked like that, too.

Kispiox lies on glacial hills covered with birches, in the mud on the east shore of the Kispiox River. The Gitksan claim they had a sprawling city, Dimlahamid, just south of there, which had to be abandoned after centuries of occupation. It sprawled for miles along the confluence of the Skeena and Bulkley rivers. Archaeologists are still looking for it, out among the birches, like Schliemann looking for Troy.

Southwest of Kispiox lies Kitwanga. Young Gitwangak mothers push their babies along the mud streets in bright, pastel-coloured carriages out of the Sears catalogue. The totems lie on their backs in the grass, staring blindly up at the sky. The young mothers laughed at me when I stopped and walked around the poles there. North of Kitwanga is the abandoned village of Kitwancool, where my uncle, Frank Leipe, would pack in when he was twenty: back then, in '51, it was still a village of longhouses and mortuary poles, falling down where they stood, smelling of smallpox and ghosts. In the cool water there he would catch huge sixty-five-pound salmon and pack them out again to the collection of rotted, abandoned log shacks and barns they called a farm, under the shadow of the Evelyn Glacier. The Skeena is a country so clean and clear you feel you have entered a dream.

To see the totems of Kispiox there in Kleinburg was like jet lag. It was like watching a movie filmed in a city you know well, and being unable to see beyond the everyday to the new city that had been made of it on the cutting floor: the exterior of one building leads to the interior of another; country roads lead off into familiar landscapes, only to end up right where you began; houses are transposed miles from their proper location; the courthouse becomes the city hall; and the whole city is mysteriously moved a half mile closer to the river. That kind of thing. In Kispiox today, the poles don't stand in front of longhouses as they did when Carr was there. They are lined up, close together, like grave-markers, where the long-houses would never have stood, rotting in the swampy ground on the shore of the river, downhill from the town. The water is cool and green. The sky lies close to the land. At the beginning of September the air smells of snow, granite, and cottonwoods. It is incredibly old. The poles are a hundred years older than the ones in Carr's paintings, and far less clumsily executed. They didn't remind me of Carr at all. Neither did they have anything in common with the highly polished poles, with the decorative adze marks, that are raised in front of government buildings throughout BC, or with the commercial welcoming figures bolted to the light poles along the main street of Duncan, in the metal and asphalt and steel and exhaust. The actual poles of Kispiox are hacked out with rocks and hand-hammered iron – there is a power of representation there that binds place and story into a unified, perceptual matrix. It is not decorative. It rises out of the wood. It speaks of great need.

In Kleinburg, art is given as a point of rest. The gallery is a shrine. The day I was there, a thin crescent moon rode above it in a sky the colour of water: clear and thin, no colour and all colours. As I stood up against the floor-to-ceiling glass and looked over the hills of maples and beeches, I stepped within the paintings and was walking through the land, weightless. It was a moment of celebration: something of nothing had been caught out of nothing and maintained as nothing – the ultimate difficulty and trial. That is life. It trembles inside our images; inside a leaf; inside a spider. It is a myth. There in Kleinburg, the state of dream had become the state of waking. The state of waking had become a dream.

I've come to Canada late! I was the rabbit rushing to the garden party. *My* watch has stopped! I feel like a refugee. In 1955 Maria came to Toronto. All through the last forty-five years, as she has raised five children and sent them off and became a poet and then a publisher, she has watched the city grow up around her, devouring farmland, transforming it into gardens and cul-de-sacs, expanding itself, growing into its dream. For most of those years, I have been in the Okanagan Valley, first as a child on the farm, and then as an adult. In the fall the sumacs flared red on the scree-and-lichen slopes. In the spring the shadbushes were white and cool. Those were years of turmoil, as our farm went bankrupt, as the colonial farming culture of the Okanagan struggled and fought to maintain some wealth and was wrenched into the modern world. All those years of struggle and bitterness and change, those years of powerlessness and defeat, when we lost the farm, when farmers lost the economic capacity to participate in the modern world, were years of growth in Toronto: change, but change accompanied by growing wealth. Our wealth.

7

COYOTE AND

THE BANKER

DO LUNCH

Change is painful, of course, but it has to happen," said Maria's son, the banker. He was sharing Thanksgiving dinner with me – a generous man. Before dinner he had practised Christmas carols on the piano downstairs, and had apologized for disturbing me – which he hadn't – when he noticed me standing behind him, listening. He was glad to be back in the family home. At dinner, he was animated. "Oh God, you're not a regionalist are you? You're not in favour of giving more power to the regions? You don't see the regions as having more say in their own affairs, do you? You're not in favour of self-sufficient economies?" He groaned good-naturedly. I think he found me a bit slow on the uptake.

"As a matter of fact," I said, "I do. I am." And then I added, in half apology, because I suddenly felt the country fool: "My experience has taught me that." I was feeling uncomfortable. I felt that regionalism was somehow the wrong thing to speak about.

I was right. "Well, look at your book," he countered in a reasonable voice, cutting his pork medallions delicately with his silver knife – pork he had cooked himself, for his parents, his family, and me. His eyes twinkled. "You couldn't get it published where you come from, so you had it published in Toronto, right?" He paused and set his knife down. His voice was even more reasonable. "You need the wealth of the city, right?" He lifted the pork to his mouth and bit it, his eyebrows raised.

"You're right."

He laughed with glee and thumped his thigh. "See! You admitted it! See there!" He looked around excitedly, like a bird, to see if anyone else had noticed.

"It's not simple, is it," I said, trying to deflect him.

People had noticed.

"Sure it's simple." He waved his fork at me instructively, chewing. "Look at the natives. They're dead, culturally. They're wiped out because their cultures were no good. Everything fits together." He swallowed and glanced over to his father, the geneticist. "Trade, humanism, commerce, industry, democracy: they are all the result of each other. That's what makes us so successful." After searching for it for a few moments, he quoted the name of a political scientist who had proven that. He looked over at his father again. His father nodded, chewing vigorously, concentrating on his food, perhaps embarrassed. The banker turned back to me. "The natives couldn't compete with that. Their culture died when it confronted our stronger culture." He took a deep slug of wine. "Mmmmm! This is good!"

Natives. At the beginning of the world, their friend Coyote walked up from the mudflats at Hope. At that time, the Fraser emptied into the sea there. Now Hope lies a hundred and sixty kilometres from salt water. It has been a long time. The world is old. Coyote walked up the Fraser Canyon and up the Thompson, one by one singing the monsters who lived there into stone. He tamed the land so that people could live there after the coming split between animals and people. For him it was an atonement for disrespect. In effect, by atoning for disrespect he created people. He *is* consciousness.

The monsters he froze are still there. They still radiate their power. They are many things: mountains along the Fraser and Thompson and Nicola Valleys, in human or half-human shape, giant, twisted – their spines broken – or on their backs, staring up at the sky; the terrors of the mind – and the self – not separated from the world, and seen there. When I stand on the windy cliffs and look across Kamloops Lake east of Savona, where the old ranchland is about to be cut up into a golf course, a resort hotel, and subdivisions of view homes, a purple mountain of demon wolves, evil and surrounded by dark clouds, howls back. I am looking a long way back into time there – back to the human equivalent of the Big Bang, the singularity at the beginning of time, where matter, space, and time are all one. We're not talking the noble savage here. We're talking about men and women scared half to death, and conquering that – and through re-routing *how* their fear flowed through the world, inventing themselves. The results were bound to be very different from those in Europe – which had to go through the same process of replacing a philosophy of creation with one of violence.

The process of colonization is not so hard to understand.

It's not something that happened long ago: the farms which a hundred years ago colonized Shuswap land are being colonized today by tiled floors, lawns, swimming pools, Jacuzzis, and golf courses – the static cast up by the city, abandoning the dialogue with the earth for images of that dialogue. They are not images of the land. They are mockeries: racy lingerie. They put the lie to the attempt to find in the earth values that can transcend the limitations of our culture and its rush to be free of the earth, the attempt to use beauty to eliminate the need for abstraction and the dual line of thought once and for all.

Tell me," says the banker. "Do you see the natives as the keepers of the waters and the stewards of the earth?"

"No. Don't be silly."

"Good." He laughs. "You haven't fallen into that trap anyway." He smiles broadly and takes another drink of my wine, smiling as it touches his lips. "I propose a toast!" he says. "To your readings next week!" Everyone echoes him, raising their glasses around the table. We drink. The wine is golden in the crystal. The cut bowls of the glasses throw golden stars of light over our hands, and over the white tablecloth as we lift them, tilt them up, and set them back down. Then the light is focussed right down the stems, into single golden-white points of light in the middle of the fluted bases, like lasers.

The taste of the vine leaves slowly evaporates in my mouth, in a summer wind.

I grew quiet. I was thinking of how, late one August, I was grafting an orchard of dwarf apple rootstocks at the foot of Fairview Mountain. I spent two days there, loping from tree to tree, one-and-a-half metres apart, in the dirt, under a sun that was like an anthill kicked open overhead and slowly falling. I took the work seriously, at twenty cents a tree, good money: building the future of the land, working with my hands. And then Ken Terbasket rode by. Back in high school, when my brother and Ken slugged it out in gym class and Ken broke my brother's nose, we called him Flash. Another young man from the band rode with him. They rode spotted Appaloosa horses and drove about sixty head of cattle before them, through the orchards. We had gone to school together for a dozen years, we shared the valley, yet we hadn't seen each other for a decade. Ken and his friend sat so easily up on their horses, their ponytails falling long and black out of the back of their dark cowboy hats. They rode past slowly. Ken laughed, "Hey! What're you doing there, crawling in the mud?"

"Grafting!" I called back. I stood up for the moment out of the pigweed, my knife in one hand, my scionwood in the other. The sun blew between us.

"What?" he called back, still riding.

"Grafting!"

"Better you than me!" he called, and waved. I laughed. It was a little ridiculous. I waved back and bent down to my work again as they rode slowly off, the cattle milling ahead of them like a slow cloud.

I thought of Barney Allison, the eighty-five-year-old chief of the band. He had been chief for longer than most of us had been alive and had become the acknowledged leader of everyone in the valley, on both sides of the border: natives, orchardists, ranchers, hippies, loggers, and the old and poor in town. He could make piercing jokes about Indians and white men that no one else could even touch. His funeral was the event of the nineties in Cawston. People came from two hundred miles around and turned normally car-free Main Street into a parking lot, blocking it completely. A food booth sprang up spontaneously along the side road by the school. It went on all night and into the next day.

I thought of how we had all started off equal in Grade 1, or so it had seemed to me, and how I had watched as the native boys dropped out of high school in Grade 8, 9, and 10, and disappeared, then reappeared in the community a decade later driving fast cars or big pickups, with long hair tightly braided and falling down their backs, and how I had felt the foundations of my life in the valley had been taken away from me – they had been based on an equality that was not there.

"Did you see my sign?!" said one young guy as I stood in his living room on the reserve. He was sitting at an Arborite table, having a cup of coffee. His kids were watching TV – on a shiny new 21-inch set that for the lack of any better TV stand was placed on top of the big old 26-inch walnut console set it had replaced.

"Yes," I said.

But I didn't reply with the appropriate conviction, for he went on to explain it: "This Spud's For You."

"Yes, I saw it." How could I help it. It was painted on four full-sized sheets of plywood and stretched a hundred feet down the barbed wire fenceline of his alfalfa field. "I'm here to buy some potatoes."

"Well, you've come to the right place!" He and his friend laughed. "Get it? This spud's for you? Like the beer!" He laughed again.

I got it.

I sat there in Toronto and said nothing of it.

I was thinking of Joe Nitsch, who had farmed grapes for Andrés Wines for a decade, across the highway from the reserve at Chopaka, before the Free Trade deal came through and the government pulled out its support for grape growing.

The idea was that by providing tariff restrictions against the import of California grapes through legislation requiring BC wineries – producers of jug wines – to use at least thirty-five percent BC grapes, a local wine industry could be encouraged, which would slowly evolve into quality production. In practice, wineries used this funding not to innovate, but to maximize profits by accepting it as a subsidy pure and simple. The irony is that the growth of a first-class wine industry came only after the removal of these tariffs. Joe was one of the eighty percent of grape growers who were disillusioned, and he used his pay-out money to get out. He has planted thirty acres of high-density apples in the old grape rows, with money from the government, and he's proud, but he's not happy.

"Damn, I went to go swimming at the bridge with the kids last night. Some young guys from the reserve told us to go home! 'Only the band can swim here from now on,' they said. I said, 'We've been swimming here for ten years!' They said, 'You whites aren't swimming here. Go home.' You know, it's not everybody. We've all been living together here for a long time. Now this. Some of the young guys are really militant. They want the whole lower valley to themselves. That's my farm, too. It's just sagebrush and rocks over here. Who wants it? What's the difference? I've helped them a lot. I've given them work. I've driven them to town. We've been friends!"

It is one of the ironies of the Canadian land reservation system that the natives of the Similkameen were given the swampy, flooded brushlands at the south of the valley and the arid benchlands surrounding them, while the upper valley, clustered around the Hudson's Bay Company post at Keremeos, open to the sun and less subject to flooding, was reserved for the whites. With the invention of electric water pumps and deep wells, this policy has left the natives with most of the good land. In the middle of the reserve a few tiny parcels are cut out, however, including Joe's. Another used to belong to the Social Credit MLA: up until 1967, the pavement coming east from Vancouver stopped right at his door. The rest of the way east to Osoyoos was gravel and dust.

I was thinking of Brandon Squakin, there in kindergarten in

Hedley: a little guy with a round face, always happy, always with a joke, always with a fresh insight, always eager – among the repressed, fragile white children of broken marriages, bikers, or just simply kids raised by their grandparents because their parents couldn't cope at all and had dumped them. Most of all, I was thinking that playing cowboys and Indians was a damned perilous thing at school when I was a boy. Half the class was native, the other half a mix of cowboys and fruit farmers. Worse yet, all the natives were cowboys. When someone called out, "Hey, all the cowboys over here! All the Indians over there!" we were always confused. By the time we had sorted it out, we were bored of the game and just had a dogpile instead. The game was more trouble than it was worth. The cowboys always said I was an Indian. The Indians always said I was a cowboy. Being neither native nor a cowboy, I always hesitated. Bad idea. Sometimes Casey Cawston, whose grandfather was the first white man to settle in the valley, and who bore the name of the town as his own – who grew up on a ranch, and would go on to ride the rodeo circuit as far as Alberta and Montana – would captain the Indian team, just to see what it was like. "You're not an Indian," he'd say to me. "Go to the other side!" But I knew I wasn't a cowboy either, and that he was. I usually walked away in frustration and disgust. This game didn't make sense at all. We were just kids together in that town. Or so I thought.

There is one man who might have been able to put the discussion into perspective: Garry Gottfriedson. Garry is a Shuswap poet from Kamloops, in the hot grasslands and burnt rock on the north side of the Thompson River: hot desert country where every road and trail is a scar and lasts longer than the life of a man – or even the lives of his children.

"I never thought of myself as a poet," he says. "I just wrote these things. For powwows sometimes. Sometimes for myself. I was doing the bush Indian thing. That's all I thought I was. That's all I thought I was good for. Then some friends sent my stuff in to a contest. They didn't tell me they'd done that. Until I won! I won a scholarship to go study with Allen Ginsberg. I didn't know Ginsberg. Who was this guy? I think Ginsberg liked that. Here were all these people crowding around him all the time, to hear what the great man was going to say, and then there I was. I got to make up my own mind. I didn't learn a lot from him, really. 'First thoughts, best thoughts.' That's what I learned. That impressed me. That one thing. Who cares if it's poetry? Who cares about theories and rules? 'First thoughts, best thoughts.' "

At the spring equinox five years ago, Garry and I gave a workshop on myth in the basement of the Church of the Emissaries of Divine Light. The Emissaries – The Lodge, as they are called here in town – started this town fifty years ago on a cattle ranch in the bush. They believe we are all descendants of angels made of fire and love. In their library they have filed *The Lord of the Rings* on the same shelf as the Bible.

Garry and I found we both looked on myth as a language, bound with the earth. We found we could agree on everything: sacred sites in the Thompson Valley, the earth as a human language, the healing power of words. "All peoples, whether they're in Europe or anywhere else, have myths," Garry said. "It's just that all these wars and invasions and this idea of higher culture have been going on for so long, people in Europe can't remember. They've lost their myths. But they have that tribal wisdom."

"Nothing's lost," I said. "The words store it. They're like little portable computers."

Garry nodded. "It's what we can save that's important now," he said. "We need to be focussed. There's no time to be angry. Now's the time when people are working to discover these things again. We have to be patient. We have to let them find their way."

Garry counts as his ancestors Cree, Shuswap, Okanagan, and Swede. He spoke of the difficulty the many poets of the Okanagan Nation have in drawing the line between the myth that is spoken and the sacred myth you do not speak of to anyone, in the way, he said, you do not speak even to your closest friend of how you make love to your wife or how it feels when she makes love to you.

"My culture was never broken," says Garry. "We were luckier than the people at the Coast, who had a longer period of contact. Our culture is an unbroken line. We just never told anyone about it."

Garry was sitting on the edge of an Arborite and metal-edged desk and began to tell the myth of Coyote, Frog, Sun, and Moon, Sun's younger brother – one of the few myths his elders had given him permission to perform.

Sun has power. When you have that power, you know it. Everything you do can be so sure. No one can take your power from you. You are solid. He struck his palm slowly with his clenched fist and held the fist and the hand together briefly before calmly washing his hands of thought, like the wings of birds above a cool lake. *In my culture women are the ones with the strongest power. Everyone knows this.*

And just as he was about to speak of how Frog grew so enraged by Moon's refusal to marry her that she leapt onto his face and clung there so strongly that they welded together and became one – Moon who now had an ugly blotch on his face, which was Frog – a door banged open, a short, fat, and grey-haired man in a long, pale grey coat came in wearing baggy pants, cameras dangling on heavy cords and straps around his neck, with his hair flying, and took two pictures without flash and left, and all of us there knew at once, without having to say a word to each other, where the line between cultural appropriation and participation had to be drawn and that the nature of that line was what we had always been trying to say.

To tell the truth, the country / city split is foreign to me. One thing I've learned from Coyote as I've suddenly found him in the bunchgrass behind the rusty barbed wire, the fence posts charred black from spring fires to clear the ditches and the edges of the fields, is that my dreams of political maturity are the same as my dreams of artistic maturity. Coyote is the same colour as the grass. At first you don't see him. Then you know all of a sudden that he's been watching you for a long time.

For twenty years I have tried to use the point of interface between art and land as a dialogue between equals. I've never believed in discarding this struggle. For a hundred years, my culture has been the boundary between the natural world and the world of cities. The Red Delicious and Bartlett pear orchards of the Similkameen are communication filters: colonial plantations looking both to enter a cultural image of wilderness and human purity, and to produce within that and out of that goods of use to the cities, whose economies they wish to enter. Like Hugh in East Kelowna, I stand in the same place as the watercolour artist interpreting a chromatic palette intuitively.

But a hundred years is a long time. I think it's time to share the wisdom gained from this experiment. Traditional history professes that the colonial system failed, and came to nothing, once the English went off cheering to war, because they did not come back to continue the mixed aesthetic and industrial image of that time. I disagree: the wars, and time, have blown over us like a cloud of neutrinos, nearly wiping us out, yet the orchards are still standing, the ranches are still flush with cattle; we are still here. Maybe the world is no longer openly asking for the wisdom we have gained, and certainly it is other wisdom than what was hoped for, and maybe the cities have even discarded the experiment as fruitless, but it has continued nonetheless. Western culture stands here in extremity. Like a space crew sent on a long journey to a distant star, who come back only to find their culture and friends and families dead for a century, it is time to face what we have done, and to speak of it, on our own terms. That is what the cities never expected. If we use the terms of a city we will fall short, for we are not the city in any pure sense.

The image of the city has been transformed here over a century of hard work and struggle into an image of the land. It is not that there is a city and a country in Canada. There are two cities.

After our workshop, Garry Gottfriedson took on the job of principal of a band school at Inkameep, among the burrowing owls, the kangaroo mice, and the vineyards. He figured it out. We have to realize it as well: this land is where we live; this is home. It has all the strength and power of any other place on earth. The alternative is to move to Vancouver or Toronto or San Francisco, or to move the values of those places to the Interior and to continue to dream of living somewhere else than where we live, and never to learn or understand the meaning or uses of honesty. It is to accept the cities as real and the earth as nothing of worth. It is to give up.

That is not evolution of thought. That is not poetry or the thousand small nuances of daily life finding their rightful place, among words. That is laziness.

Poetry, for instance, has in BC become travel writing. The Cariboo is presented as a cute and cuddly wild west. "Though now accessible and to a certain measure tamed, this vast region offers a sense of what it was." Do you understand that? "It is an area closer than you think and more removed than you can imagine." Advertising copywriters get away with this kind of stuff all the time. My favourite, though, has to be the special on golfing in the Okanagan. "Tee off in a working orchard at Kelowna's nine-hole McCulloch Orchard Greens Golf Club. Historic orchard equipment is even displayed at the ninth hole!" It sounds great, alright. Except that of the four hundred and fifty acres of that orchard, just about every single acre was removed from orcharding to put up the golf course. And then there's the stump: an old Wealthy tree, cut off four feet from the ground and ringed with a perfect, circular stone wall three feet high – very funereal, solemn. They must have pulled out ten thousand apple trees to put in the golf course. In that stony East Kelowna land, that's a tough job – even harder than planting them in the first place with a shovel and a pick. I guess in the end they just couldn't bear to pull out one more tree. The greatest irony is that this orchard was the home orchard of the pivotal orchard company in the Okanagan – and the best orchard land, to boot. That's why they chose it for their home lot: commercial orcharding in BC started there. The land *is* of historic importance. Unfortunately, this business about the pseudo-history at the ninth hole, the old and clumsy machines somehow removed from us, patronizing and slightly cute – a wooden-tanked sprayer, a cutting plow, a couple of disc harrows – probably about one percent of the equipment needed to run that orchard and only made obsolete by the installation of the golf course – is advertising material paid for by the government. Thanks a lot, guys! With friends like you …

S imilarly, when the government set out to bring peace and political predictability to a land-use decision process played out in the media with dramatic confrontations between environmentalists, labour, and large corporations, they asked parties interested in the forests to sit down together and achieve consensus. Logging companies, ranchers, miners, loggers, environmentalists, hotel operators, local government representatives, and hunting guides joined this process, which quickly devolved into a newspaper fight. On one hand the Cariboo Communities Coalition – pro-logging – paid for full-page ads of young families looking responsible and troubled, as they no doubt were, hunkered down in front of their trucks; Weldwood paid for ads about forestry responsibility – a dock, a pristine lake, a ring of black trees, a late evening sky, a way of life, and the statements that we can continue to log ("harvest," if you don't mind) at our present rate – 115 percent of the sustainable yield – forever. On the other hand, the environmentalists – these guys actually quoted figures – claimed that we have seven and one half years left, then nothing for five years, and then 85 percent of the current (exceeded) sustainable yield. Who're we to believe? Anybody: this is just about images – our real lives are lived in confusion and silence. To open *that* silence is the revolution. That's one of the problems with saying that the Cree and Haida and Carrier were inferior because they did not invent steam engines: you get trapped in the language of steam engines. When the editor of the *100 Mile Free Press* went to the Ministry of Forests office and sat down there over a cup of coffee and asked who he was supposed to believe, the forests manager just shrugged: *he* didn't know! When the federal government proposed putting in five new parks in the Chilcotin, their last chance to protect five endangered ecosystems in BC, the head forester of Ainsworth Lumber was quick to point out that they had just built a hundred-million-dollar oriented strand board plant in 100 Mile House, and those scrubby little slow-growing high-altitude pines, two hundred miles away across the Fraser River, were just the sort of trees they were set up to harvest. There is no way to argue with that, because the vocabulary is too tightly controlled.

The work of a fly-fisherman, fashioning a grasshopper out of deer hair and walking miles along the cutbanks of the Thompson River north of Lytton, among the old, abandoned villages with their graves and dead fruit trees, and casting out through the blue air so the hopper lies like a breath upon the cool water, is the basis for building a culture.

The change can be made. Rob Dawson gave up a life as a lawyer to return to the Similkameen and farm his father's big orchard above the swamps and cattle ranches at Similkameen Station. It was on that orchard that my father got his start farming, and there I lived until I was four, in the manager's house, looking out through the elms to the swamps and willowbrakes of the reserve. In the summer, as the evening light cuts in horizontally under the western clouds, you can sit there and watch ants mate five hundred feet above the pastures: clouds of tiny white stars, hanging there, while below them long distorted shadows spill over the ground.

The heir of my father's position as spokesman for change and growth in the BC fruit industry, Rob remarks: "Farmers know what's going on. They have all the time in the world to think. A university professor, or a consultant, or anyone who gets paid to think, spends a lot of time sitting in front of a computer: writing reports, teaching, writing memos. That's not creative. There's only an hour or two every day left over for thinking. You can't get much done in that time. But a farmer spends the whole day outside. He has the mountains around him, and the sun. He's standing in the wind. He's out there in the rain. He's doing boring repetitive tasks that he's done a million times before. He's pruned so many trees, he doesn't pay attention to them anymore. He's on automatic pilot. If he wasn't, he would go nuts. So he does nothing but think. He thinks about the world, for ten hours a day. Nobody else has that kind of time. If you want to understand the world, ask a farmer. He knows what's going on. You know, I've replanted my orchard. I've spent a million bucks. Maybe I'll get it back. Maybe I won't. But we all have to do it. It's a gamble, but you have to try. You have to make a decision and go with it, and hope it's the right one. Otherwise you know exactly where you're going: nowhere. Extinct."

Jim is an example of what Rob meant. Jim is a gentle man who would rather be riding his horse, decked out in silver and leather, in Omak or Merritt or Winthrop, than out pruning his trees. Two years ago he looked up from where we were pruning an old snag of a red-limbed apricot tree. It was early March, a week after our friend and neighbour Larry had died suddenly in his wife's arms. Fifty of us were there to help out Larry's son and widow. A high sky burned blue and thin above Jim's red hair – it was snowing on Goat Mountain to the south, above and just behind the valley ridge. We were below that cold air. All around us the valley was brown and full of wind. After a decade of struggle, of drifting apart, of driving trucks of fruit into the North, into Alberta, or down to the Coast, of watching our families crack or turn bitter or cynical or even break apart, we had come together for a few hours. We were a community. Those two days we worked together with a strength we had never known before. Among Larry's tangled trees we seemed to float just off the ground. He had been wrestling with them for two decades. Now the struggle had come to an end. It was a truce: the trees showed all the angular cuts and the scars, and had the red bark of frost and neglect; Larry had a sudden, massive stroke. The trees were a tangled record of struggle. The wind blew through them and came out all chopped up and sharp.

Just two days before, a fighter jet had roared up over the border. Where it had come from we did not know, but we all figured it must have come from the old nuclear bomber base in the bunchgrass and ponderosa pines just outside of Spokane: twenty air minutes through the deserts and then the high forests of the Indian land to the southeast. Wherever it came from though, it circled above town at five hundred feet altitude, then roared back down the valley and out again into the Columbia. The air boomed and cracked behind it, and echoed back and forth upon itself between the narrow valley walls. Everyone ran out of their houses and stared up, but the plane was already gone.

"The Americans are smart," Jim said, up in the 'cot tree. "They're waiting until we're so broke we can't operate anymore. Then California's going to come up and say, 'Hey, look guys: we'll make you a deal you can't refuse. We'll put all your debt on our books. Just give us all your water.' Just watch. It'll happen. They have an economy. They can absorb that. It's nothing to them. It's the whole population of Canada there. It makes me mad. They don't need to attack us. They just slowly break us down, and then move in and say they've saved us." He was getting himself worked up. He stopped pruning, thrust his boot up against the trunk to support himself, and started to talk quickly, but very quietly. "God, you know, this is an invasion of our airspace. We're the only ones who know these guys are here. The Canadian Air Force certainly doesn't. He's below radar level. We have to take matters into our own hands. We have the right to do that. Maybe we should do what those Afghanis have done." The rest of us had stopped pruning and stood around under the tree, listening. Jim was clambering through the central bowl of the tree by then, cutting out suckers, and talking, almost to himself but not quite, honestly and bluntly, and still very quietly. "We need some SAM missile batteries out here among the trees, and the next time one of those bastards comes over the border we'll blow him out of the air. We have to take things into our own hands."

We were all completely silent, in a rough ring around the tree, clippers in our hands, saws in our back pockets, staring.

I was burning the branches of my pine tree today, the one the ants had hollowed out, the one the woodpecker loved all summer, cocking his head and listening intently – like a fourteen-year-old kid with a Walkman – then driving his beak in suddenly and hard, an extension of his hearing: focussed; pure will. On the bed of coals I threw the butt of the tree, a two-inch slice I had made so my kids and the neighbour's kids could count the rings: fifty-eight years old. Not long. Cattle must have grazed around it when it sprouted among the wild geraniums and paintbrush. After five minutes of smoke pouring out of the ant-holes in that stump, directly on the red-hot coals, the wood began to smoke. The bark had already flashed off. I lifted the butt with my pitchfork and flipped it over. To my amazement, the carpenter ants stepped out of the wood: fast, black, purposeful. They moved quickly outwards, like soldiers clambering out of trenches after a bombardment and through the smoking field of no-man's land, like the GIs lined up and then sent walking towards ground zero in Nevada, while the fireball was still pouring up and the sun had become a mouth, swallowing them, as the wind whipped around them, picking up the gritty sand and dragging it into the fire. I watched with awe. With that kind of strength, you could survive a forest fire, easy. You could take over the world.

8

WITH SALMAN

RUSHDIE IN

KING CITY

To explore the possibility that our urban and rural cultures have become so separated that a dialogue between them is no longer possible, I asked Heather what she saw as the relationship between a city, its suburbs, and the rural land around it. She lived in the city, after all. And it was, after all, Thanksgiving: a harvest festival. And the city was devouring the country. That didn't look like a conversation. It looked like a siren song. I figured this was the right thing to be talking about. I asked because I knew what I thought about life on the land: that it is a process of attention, the gathering of a gift, and a strict focus on life. On the land you use *life* as a building block; only after that do you use ideas. What Heather thought about it I did not know, but I knew it was equally important.

"I'm not qualified to talk about that," she said. "I've never given it much thought." She sounded hurt.

"That's an answer in itself," I said. "There's really not much need to say anything else." I hoped that smoothed things over, but I doubted it.

So I sat there in a Volkswagen Golf driving out of Toronto, with a battery running down second by second because of a shot alternator, trying to make a bridge with a woman who spoke a different language. As we drove, I developed the disturbing feeling that there in Toronto, the magic city had completely replaced both harvest and loam with technological substitutes, and that the languages were now so different that little could be transferred between the city and the land: despite all we shared, there was no chance of a conversation, nor of a shared consciousness created by that conversation, that was not fundamentally derailed before it began. Nonetheless, I was hoping that the survival, in a strong sense, in the suburbs, of a myth of "country" life indicated that the dialogue was still essential, only that it had its own peculiarly urban terms.

The question was important to me. Farming could not be the only way to relate to the earth. That made no sense. I was looking for some perspective. I had just returned from a summer in the Bavarian Alps – tourist country: conservative, sentimental, tough. Standing on the top of the ski jump in Partenkirchen and looking down at the amphitheatre below and the concrete seats where Goering and Hitler sat at the Olympics in 1936, I had come to realize that moreso than all the wars that have been fought in its name, this romanticism, this *Harrowsmith* image of "The Country," this rural idea of *Volk*, is the definition of the twentieth century and the basis of modern urbanized life around the world. I wanted to get a better handle on it. "Perhaps it has to do with kitsch," I thought, as unknown to Heather and me the battery was draining lower and lower. I was thinking of the hundred woodcutter shops in Oberammergau. A small city of tourists pours into that town every day. Everyone is eager to touch this country charm – this true definition of the human. When I was there, I saw an American army major sprint from his minivan, with his wife and kids running behind him and a video camera over his shoulder, to get to the shops, fast. I turned and watched him. He ran well!

Three years ago in August, I told this over the phone to Ron Hatch, the publisher of my fruit-growing memoir, *Out of the Interior*. He sat in his living room in Vancouver, with an electronic device clamped to his leg: under house arrest. He had allowed himself to be arrested, protesting the logging of Clayoquot Sound on the west coast of Vancouver Island, so that he could use his position as an English professor at UBC to present a coherent, logical argument in court. But he wasn't allowed to speak.

"It's enough to make you lose your illusions about humanity," I said.

"Who said," he answered characteristically, dryly, "that I have any illusions about humanity?"

Right.

If not kitsch, I considered further, then maybe it had to do with reducing artifacts and images of use, like pitchforks and wood-handled scythes, to a readily marketed state of contemplation, hung on the walls of restaurants, without, sadly, the deep thought that comes from use – the work of a man with the tools that extend the range of his body, like an old man scything on a steep alpine slope, my grandfather at sixty-eight years of age building a racing sloop out of mahogany and teak and spar varnish, or the work I did with Wayne on the vineyards of the Similkameen, cutting out the four-foot-tall pigweeds with a bush scythe when the weed-spraying program broke down, the steel wet with sap, a thin layer of dust collecting as mud against the back ridge of the stiff and stubby blade.

My question was meaningless to Heather.

She did not even understand the question. The fact that I asked it caused her obvious pain.

I sit on the shore of a high plateau lake. The grasses and naked aspens around me are white with hoarfrost. Never before have I felt the world to be so quiet, and so still. From an urban perspective, nothing is happening here, yet from a rural perspective, nothing is happening here either. We are at a crossroads. I stand in the stillness and look both ways: back to the farmers, clamouring for subsidy as the world of industrial trading defeats their efforts to leave it, and forward to the cities, where it is possible to gain the perspective to write poetry and see the land (and yet impossible to leave the city), and for the first time in years I realize again that I am tired of false choices: I am tired of tinkering; I am tired of judgement. I want a new civilization. I want it, because everything is alright. Everything that is alive is alright. We don't have to choose; we have to talk to each other about what concerns us deeply.

On my last day in Toronto, the trees turned red. I wasn't even looking for them. It was more than I had ever expected, and more than either Heather or Maria had described. No wonder they had tried so hard to bring the trees and me together. We have maples in the Interior, too, of course – Rocky Mountain maples, growing in rocky streambeds in the mountains: small splashes of colour reflecting in fast water. In Toronto, though, it was as if the trees were formed of light and breath. The earth had become heaven. It was radiant. The sun paled.

On that last day, Heather and I had driven to Timothy Eaton's old stone mansion. Below its leaded French doors the red trees reflected in the grey water of the lake – in turn reflecting the thin, high cloud. In a low red-brick building sprawling along the shore across from the frilly gothic stonework, I spoke to a group of nineteen-year-old security guards. For this I had flown across the country. I tried to make it worthwhile for them. I was there because their instructor, lost in the low expectations of the community college system, had given them a choice between report writing and creative writing. They chose the latter. It seemed a frivolous choice. I was doubtful.

I wasn't the only one. "Don't be put off if some of them get up halfway through," Maria had said the night before. "They have jobs they have to get to."

"Ha!" laughed her husband, the geneticist, sipping from a bowl of soup. "If you see them lift their billy clubs, don't worry! 'Excuse me,' they'll say. 'I just have to go bash in a few heads now.'"

They sure were young. Their instructor had them stand and read their poems back to me: childish work, written to Grade 3 expectations, and not very demanding ones at that.

It made me angry. Some things never change. We have managed to build nothing with literature except an expectation we are unwilling to meet. It made Heather even more angry. Four young men lounged in their heavy down jackets in the corner and poked each other and whispered and fell over each other while crushing a Nestlé's iced tea tin. I was back in high school. The teacher wore a yellow pin: I AM SALMAN RUSHDIE.

"I like your pin," I said.

"It was given out by PEN," she answered. She shrugged. I looked at her: curly blond hair, long flowing flowery dress. She didn't look like Salman Rushdie. Good disguise!

Given that Rushdie was there, and these were police officers of the future, I read my poem about murder. Tough stuff. "You see, there was this French girl. She came to town for a few days' work on the farms. Then she disappeared. The police found her three months later, buried in the greenhouse, but without her head. Everyone felt they knew who the killer was, the farmer next door, but they couldn't prove it. The talk of the town was that without a head they could make no positive ID, so there was no case. It dragged out for a year. The women in town were all frightened, and the men all set their jaws and became quiet." I read:

> There was nothing to understand,
> the men thought. It's as easy as changing the oil in the
>   tractor
> every 300 working hours or putting on a pot of coffee,
> feeling there was some shame
> in understanding.

I explained that violence is a human trait; that it doesn't do us any good to simply ascribe it to an individual, then to banish him or her. I said that we had to claim responsibility for it. That didn't do much for them. OK. So I read them my poem about religious persecution. I had written it two weeks before the sentence of death fell on Rushdie. The poem is one of those things I write every year at the winter solstice, bringing the year together. This one went further than most. "Visiting Yeats," I called it. It assessed my life in literature and how little it had achieved if I did not somehow break out of the ghetto of literature and speak about the world. It is in the world that decisions are made about literature, after all, not in literature. Action is the corollary to contemplation.

"Although all my poems are spiritual," I told the cops, "there are other spiritual forces in town, conservative and even right-wing Christian sects, who would burn my books if they ever came to power." Love is not a desired characteristic everywhere. "As an old man," I explained, "Yeats could walk through the Municipal Gallery in Dublin and see all his friends from the Irish Revolution, and could give thanks that he knew them, but I had to go to the unheated room down my hall and sit with my books in the cold. Not what could be called a shrine." I read on: how, outside, the land was being stolen from us; how dogs – bad dogs – roamed free, black in the night streets. That didn't do much for them either. Sorry, Salman.

OK, I thought. They aren't that kind of police officer. They were only nineteen. I read them "Canadian Backyard Sex," about artificial insemination of bees: tiny stirrups, plastic tubes, syringes, and the delicacies of squeezing the heads of drone bees until their semen spurted out. "The queens like to do it with about seventeen guys," I read. They perked up. They watched my lips. They didn't say a thing. They didn't even touch the Nestlé's tin. The women blushed, nervous, beautiful. That was more like it. The teacher sat among them in the back, Salman shining away on her lapel, smiling. Heather sat in the exact middle of the room, with the students spreading around her. She cradled a dozen books in a cooking pot box. "It's more discreet," she had said, as we walked in across the parking lot. "If you carry books around like this, it isn't threatening." VISIONS COOKSET BY CORNING, said the box.

"Poetry is threatening?" I had asked.

"Harold," she had said, fixing me with a level gaze. "It is very threatening."

W e went for a drink in Timothy's house. The bar was closed. Most of the tables had been carried away. Dust and torn-up paper napkins were strewn over the floor. We had to hunt up some chairs. Salman Rushdie was embarrassed. Eventually she went out and asked the receptionist to mix us a drink. We sat with a student on a work-study program from the University of Waterloo, who was working there as a tutor. "God, the quality of writing is going downhill here every year," he said. He said many things – a passionate set of pronouncements. I remembered those days well, having long arguments with my father, in which I quoted Ezra Pound about poets and artists being the antennae of the race, setting up the language, showing everybody else what to think. Nutty stuff. My father would get very upset.

"No one tells me what to think!" he'd bellow.

"Well, it's not that," I'd say, but I never could figure out what it really was, apart from my need to belong to a company of peers whose worth mattered. That my parents and I intensely shared a culture and the land and needed each other, I had not yet learned to see.

"Why do you write such long titles?" the tutor asked, thumbing through my book.

"It's fun," I said.

"Some of these are really long." He flipped back a few pages and held the book out to me. "Look at this one! The title is longer than the poem!" "Four Dimensional Asthma: A Parker Brothers' Game."

Some executive in a crisp suit, at Timothy's for a conference, wandered in and looked around uncertainly. His name was printed on a white index card, which hung around his neck on a length of butcher cord. This was the way you treat the insane, or young children you send somewhere alone on the train. I thought of *The Secret Garden*. We stared at him. He left.

"What do you like to read?" I asked, lowering my eyes. The tutor named some short-story writers I had never heard of. Good. This was the way it's supposed to be. Everything's OK. And then he said:

"I'm supposed to read Joyce, but I just can't. I can't read *Dubliners*."

"Why not?" snapped Heather, suddenly alert.

"I can't be bothered."

"But you have to read Joyce," she said. "He is important."

"I don't want to. It's all so obvious."

"It wasn't!" She sat there, with her jaw hanging down, and then closed her mouth before she said anything else. Her eyes burned.

"I took courses at Waterloo," I said. "By correspondence."

"I hate correspondence courses!" he said. "That's not a real education."

Now *I* was on the defensive. "I had no other options. I had to learn what I needed wherever I could. It was great."

"What did you study?" he asked.

"Classical Greek. German language."

He looked at me with pity.

"I write short stories," he said.

"Do you ever try to get them published?" I asked.

"No. I keep them in my desk. I write them for myself. That makes me happy. I have no desire for fame."

I nodded. I smiled.

Another man in a suit stepped in. His name hung around his neck. He looked lost. I stared at him.

As we drove back from Timothy's, Heather explained to me about the Ontario community college system. "It sets low sights for its students," she said. "They didn't make it into university. They are second best. That's what people think. Nonsense!" "God, wasn't it funny," she said. "That awful room. And we asked the guy sweeping the floor if the bar was open, and he said, 'I dunno,' and then looked up and saw no one behind the bar and said, so politely, 'Nope,' and kept on sweeping." She was angry. This wasn't an education. It was a waste of time: the young man there from Jamaica, with the beautiful deep musical voice, was writing poor imitations of Auden's clipped and frozen love rhymes from the thirties. They were bad when Auden wrote them. If this young guy had just spoken with his own voice, I would have sat down among the young security guards and listened to him for as long as I could. I would have stayed there for hours. He just needed to talk in his own voice. It was sad. No one was helping him – no one who had found out by imitating Auden how bad Auden could write when he wrote badly. I'd been there. I recognized the problem immediately. Poor bugger!

And yet, his tutor, the academic elite, spoke of Rousseau and said with pride that the Victorian poets were his favourites. He didn't like anything written after Matthew Arnold.

Maybe that kid from Jamaica was right on track: fifty years ahead of his time.

The car died in the middle of North York. There was no way to know that we were in North York and not somewhere else in the endless grid that is Toronto, except by the signs along the road: WELCOME TO NORTH YORK, THE CITY WITH A ♥. "Well, it didn't die far out," Heather said, stepping out, agitated. I had just pushed the car off the main road and into a sidestreet. We stood there and stared at it. "I'll have to get it towed," she said. As we stood there, an old woman suddenly appeared beside us in the dusk.

"Excuse me," she said softly. She looked frightened and frail beneath her puffy blue permed hair. "Would either of you two be able to change a quarter? The man on the bus wouldn't let me on because I didn't have exact change." She was trembling, fighting back her tears.

"Of course," I said. Heather and I dug in our wallets and found two dimes and a nickel. We traded them for the old woman's quarter. She passed it over to us like a wafer at communion, with great care: an item of immense value.

"God bless you both," she said. She slipped off slowly into the dusk.

I felt blessed.

"Is that standard on buses?" I asked. Heather nodded.

I dropped the hood with a bang. We walked across the street and into the North York Public Library to use the phone. Inside, it was bright and warm. "I'm technically supposed to ask you if you have a quarter for the payphone," the woman said behind the counter: oak; very nice. Heather pursed her lips and shook her head.

With a bored expression, the woman handed over the phone.

Maria and I went up the CN Tower, for Roland's sake. "Look at that," said Maria, staring straight down. "There are hardly any train tracks. When we first came to Toronto the tracks went forever down here. No one ships anything by train anymore. It's all truck traffic out in the suburbs." I stared out over the blue water and the long curve of the lake. It looked like the sea. It looked like an afternoon with A.Y. Jackson. It took my breath away: the Group of Seven were real. Maybe Champlain wasn't such pointless history after all. I looked the other way: electronic circuits and memory chips and CPUs stretched to the horizon, big memory stacks stood evenly spaced across the entire grid, and in the middle of it all, big jets landed and took off, like shuttles at a space dock.

You're right, Roland. It's big.

I stood on a sheet of glass and stared down between my feet at the train tracks far, far below. All around me young men were dragging and pushing their shrieking girlfriends out onto the glass. I threaded through them and bought a postcard of the tower standing in a purple sky and being struck by a long curl of lightning. "Poet gets struck down on the tower!" I wrote on the back with a ballpoint pen, and drew a little picture of myself on top of the tower, with little bolts sticking out of my neck. As we came down in the high-speed elevator, we all swallowed hard. "You get used to it after a while," the attendant said, looking painfully bored. He focussed on absolutely nothing. An old man shook his head slowly, firmly, from side to side. His cheeks trembled. A baby cried.

W hat a place. Somewhere between the young man in the green uniform who gave out parking tickets, with enough violations to keep him in a sweat (the fine was the same amount as the unpaid parking – and a lot more convenient), and the nosebleed I had at an Italian restaurant because I had naively said "Yes" when the waitress asked if I'd like black pepper with my pasta, I was really happy there in Toronto. The waitress had smirked. I had just thought the offer was a little bit of urban style. Ha! It's true, though: this big concrete city had made me unexpectedly happy. And why not: for ten percent of us, this is Canada. Here was a form of urban planning that worked. It was not new to me: I had seen it before, all over BC, in cities like Langley and Kelowna and Salmon Arm and Castlegar and Williams Lake, where it devolved into long plastic strip malls and suburbs like modules dropped from a cargo plane. In Toronto, though, it was complete: a city that had risen to rule the country; an electronic processor; a fax-modem – our real capital; a temple city. Being there was like being at Chichén Itzá in its prime. It was like a novel by Salman Rushdie: to get to this magic city, I got to fly across Canada – a strange and exotic land. Sure, I knew a bit about it, through TV, books, and most of all through supermarket and CIBC calendars: each month graced with a picture, of a fishing village in Nova Scotia; a wheatfield in Saskatchewan (thunderclouds on the horizon above fields of golden wheat and a threshing machine working overtime to get through it before the sky breaks); a lake in the Rockies, reflecting white-and-blue peaks; a Toronto skyline; old Quebec City, with a black carriage; fishing boats at the wharf in Tofino; cairns in the tundra; bears fishing in the Yukon River; a covered bridge in New Brunswick; a rocky shore in Newfoundland, with a few small beached wooden boats – one picture for every province. It was better than a novel by Salman Rushdie. And I got to fly there with a lot of men in black and grey suits and $300 leather briefcases, and a few women in black capes with $400 eelskin briefcases. The men made crude sexual jokes. The women pretended not to hear. I felt embarrassed. I looked out of place, too, with my torn Naugahyde pouch and my coil ring notebook: MADE IN INDONESIA, HILROY CO. TORONTO, stamped crudely across the cover. I felt that at any moment someone was going to come up to me, tap me on the shoulder, and say, "Excuse me. You'll have to leave now." Despite my unease, it was great to be among those people. They hurried. They ran. They sprinted, like Ben Johnson, down the corridors of the airport. Some of them speed-walked. They were good. They were really good. It was a frenzied movement of people and energy: someone had sped up the videotape. These were people who had somewhere to be, an hour ago. No one rushes like that in the Cariboo. There in the Toronto airport, I got to sit for a few hours among the temple priests and priestesses. I watched them stuff their last papers into their cases and snap the locks shut. They looked up, furtively. Too busy to smile, they frowned. The stewardesses called them "Sir" and "Ma'am."

As the plane flew over the grid of the city, then over the rural grid which it had replaced perfectly, and over the sandy estuaries of slow, muddy flatland rivers pouring into the turquoise water, and over the Great Lakes, for the first time in my life I saw our world hanging in space, like a drop of dew. Hour by hour red forests and thin farms spilled out far below. Then we cruised through a ceiling of cloud at 29,000 feet. The earth curled away in a perfect globe. The sky above the plane was an unearthly bright blue. There was a lemon yellow sheen on the horizon. I smelled the sun. It smelled like forever.

From Calgary I took a little plane back to Kamloops. We taxied out, a gnat among the 747-200s and the Airbuses, then suddenly we were climbing above the city and tearing through the air towards the Rockies: very small. It sounded like we were riding a lawnmower. It seemed like we would never get to the mountains: they were beyond the edge of the world. They rose up on the edge of the prairie, a wall of ice and stone, blue and white, blowing with wind. We got there, though, suddenly and quickly, and we were over them. They foamed below us, and then there was BC, my country, crumpled land, like someone had squashed a beer can with his fist: the white area on the map, with a question mark in the middle of it, in India ink. We landed in that question mark, in a reek of sulphur hanging low over the river from the pulp mill. I suddenly realized: there was no smell in Toronto. Toronto didn't smell like anything at all. I had expected a big, industrial city. I rediscovered my old Apple IIE. Of course. Computer systems have to run free of dust.

I sit on the shore of a high plateau lake. The grasses and naked aspens around me are white with an inch of hoarfrost. Never before have I felt the world to be so quiet, and so still. The wind buffets my face as I watch the coots swim in slow circles on the graphite face of the lake. The fog blows up around them into the air and drifts west in slow thin clouds. Every cloud has the same volume, determined by the molecular density of the air: when they reach a certain size the wind catches them, each one the same, and drags them away. The world is ancient. As I stand here among my iris beds, I have an answer now for the banker who asked at Thanksgiving if I was a regionalist, and smiled when I said, "Of course I am." My answer is: we are all the city. No one gets to define alone what it is, because no one is it alone.

It was like my friend Brad Bain, the antique dealer. A trader in Nazi military pins from Winnipeg, he had sold a heritage house in Winnipeg (for next to nothing) and had bought a singlewide trailer by the river in Keremeos (for more than it was worth) to take part in a farming life, and to have a garden and a few chickens. He had cut out lace curtains to put up in the chicken pen, to needle me. In the end, he was unable to kill a single bird. When one of his peahens froze its foot in the winter, he amputated the foot neatly at the knuckle with his fish-filleting knife and cauterized the wound with a blowtorch. The bird screeched horribly, but all next summer as Brad was out on the dike fly-fishing among the cicadas, it hopped around on its one foot, around the chicken run and out under the cherry trees and the carpet of fallen, wormy cherries dropped by the robins. It seemed to get along alright.

"I'll tell you what I'd do with that stupid bird, if it was mine," my father-in-law said. "That's cruel." His jaw clenched. Finally he went over there and did it.

There was couchgrass in Brad's irises, and the black rhizomes of couchgrass threaded right through the tubers of his spuds.

"God, you're not an old hippy, are you?" Brad had asked, all of a sudden, as we talked about the seventies in the valley while I was showing him how to prune his fruit trees.

"Isn't everyone?" I had asked back, suddenly realizing as I said it that, no, everyone is not.

To the banker, my answer is this: I have watched our trees fall. I have watched our people replaced with machines, and yes, that is profit for cities such as Toronto, but profit only for those parts of *this* place that fit into the grid. And what's that? Ten percent of our lives? Let's be generous: twenty percent? Not insignificant, but eighty percent is not insignificant either. I have seen money flow in, to be used to build nothing except houses and roads. When the trees are gone, when the gold is gone, when the farms are subdivided, there is nothing left. There is nothing quaint about Hedley. It is just simply very real. I have, in short, lived my whole life where the cultural wealth of industry – concerts, theatre, music, books – the profit for cities such as Toronto, the payback, are slight, if not non-existent, and where movies are all violent, misogynistic, and trite.

The banker said, "Don't you see: for every job lost, there is one created in making that machine?"

Well, yes, maybe there is, but those are jobs that tend to distance us further and further from the earth, and allow us less and less to work with our hands and to teach each other, to remain a community and to extend our culture. If you can't accept that, there really is no conversation.

When I was a kid there were three mills in Keremeos, with beehive burners pouring sparks into the night. Now there is just a big mill an hour away in Okanagan Falls, and no trees left, and another mill in Penticton, with piles of logs at the front and giant claw-mouthed loaders, like big yellow stag-horn beetles, and grey, rotting piles of finished lumber in the back: a pure definition of industrial purpose. For Keremeos, this idea of rationalization, centralization, and jobs created in the manufacturing of new machinery is a disaster. For Keremeos and for the country as a whole, there is no gain at all (except perhaps a rise in the welfare rolls), only a transfer of power. People come to Keremeos now to retire – from what? From life? Moving to a farming valley is a retirement from life? Something only the wealthy can do, with their treasury bills and IBM stock?

A friend of mine in 100 Mile House, Doug, is a welder. He works for Exco. They manufacture automated sawmill and logging equipment for Ainsworth Lumber. "This stuff is the best there is," he says. "Nobody's better than Ainsworth. No one's more automated. We invented all this stuff. We have a machine that can cut three trees, one at a time, hold them, then set them down on a neat pile and cut three more, without stopping. We have another machine that'll strip a hundred-foot tree of branches in ten seconds. People used to do all that work. We export complete mill lines to new plants all over the US. We've just shipped a complete plant to Florida. But it makes you sick. The only future for the logging industry is for guys like me to lose their jobs. I mean that: every time we ship a machine out, we all take our hard hats off and stand there with our heads bowed" – he mimes holding his hard hat to his chest – "for the poor bastard who's just lost his job."

Ninety percent of all the trees ever cut in BC have been cut in the last fifteen years. During the same time, 25,000 jobs have been lost. They have not been replaced with anything. The pressure to log the rainforest of the Clayoquot was based on the need to preserve one hundred and twenty jobs for ten years. Don't believe it. It has nothing to do with jobs or loggers. Nothing.

That's just a photograph of a mountain lake.

When you stand under a towering Douglas fir and feel the water rising up past you into the sun, you don't speak *that* language.

It's time we really talked.

It was after Christmas when *Titanic* came to town. The temperature had dipped to thirty below outside, in the ice and squeaking snow of the parking lot. Inside the sprawling old Rangeland Theatre the temperature was hovering around the freezing mark. The ice cubes in the soda drinks were still there at the end of the show, clinking long after the Coke and Sprite were gone. There under a sky of water-stained acoustic tile, with the equally water-stained purple-and-gold curtains, a good night's crowd usually consists of thirty people, scattered lightly throughout the theatre. On any given night, greetings are called out across the hall, and people turn backwards in their chairs to pick up conversations with their friends a few rows back. The floors are sticky with spilled pop. When I say friends, I don't mean young people. To be thirty years old in 100 Mile is to be incredibly young. Almost everyone under that age is living in Vancouver, Kamloops, and Calgary. We export them at the rate of a hundred and twenty a year – pretty well the entire high-school graduating class. In Vancouver, though, there are young people, with their verve and style and drive and beauty. When I'm there, I have to fight down the urge to run up and give them a hug and say, "Thank you! Just for being you."

But when *Titanic* came to town, the theatre was packed. Three hundred and fifty people were jammed in the three hundred and fifty seats that night, and, remarkably, almost the entire audience was between the ages of nineteen and twenty-five. The place was wild with laughter and a roar of conversation, hands held, cheeks kissed, enthusiastic waves, greetings shouted out across the rows, everyone catching up on each other's lives – one giant family reunion. Everyone had come home for Christmas. And then, four days later, they all left town.

As I watch a tundra swan swim slowly among the brown and glowing reeds out by the muskrat house, I know that an economy built on replacement may be fine for Toronto, but it's terrible for people who live here and want to stay and are being replaced. There's no dignity in living a life that you can never be a part of, to have nothing to give your children. There's no humanity in that. It's like the run-down working-class trailer courts of 103 Mile and Winfield and Olalla looking at the lush 4,000-square-foot log homes that Germans and Vancouver or Calgary lawyers dreaming of a life in the wilderness build with commanding views of the valleys: you see your powerlessness very, very clearly.

It is, I believe, what the families owning stories of Coyote call theft.

L et's be honest: if you side with the earth, you share the fate of the earth. That's pretty sobering. It means that to care for ourselves we have to care for the earth. But it's good, you know. It's good, because we have lived here on the land for a long time, and have learned much. What we have learned is that we have communal cultural wealth – in the specific way the machine technologies of cities are the cultural wealth of those who live among them. We are not really poor at all. What wealth we have, however, is unspoken: weather, joy, grief, pain; the snow that blasts in horizontally over the brown fields when in just a few hours the lakes turn from steel blue to jet black, hard, scoured clean by wind, and the cattle trample their hay underfoot into the mixed mud and snow, and cowboys move through them in their black slickers, like astronauts on the moon seen on a flickering screen – all the cattle and horses splashed across the bunchgrass, with snow blowing over them like electrons out of a photon tube. Men and women move through the storm, steady and strong, working. People came here a long time ago to meet the land, and they have met it. They are exhilarated with it. What they have met, however, the earth, beyond any concept of land or beauty, does not fit in with what Toronto has become, and thus is invisible to people in Toronto. Sadly, as the cowboys and loggers live here within the economy and official culture of Toronto, it is often invisible to them, too. So instead of their wealth, the moon spilling cold through November pines, they see the poverty, that part of their lives – perhaps ten percent – which is a poor version of Toronto: the broken down houses of Lac La Hache, the forests they must cut down to pay for their big trucks and their barrels of 90W industrial lube and their satellite dishes, the library of 100 Mile House with hardly any books for children.

S o, what is to be done?
  You can dismiss the civilization of the land as an unsuccessful experiment that led only to the expensive and bankrupting infrastructure of empire – unsustainable – or you can accept it as a successful one which has moved past the cities and has discovered information which is of human value and use. Either way, however, it is not inevitable that we make the land into a city as Toronto or Vancouver are cities, as exciting as they may be. That is an old thing. It has been done. We have the opportunity to make something new. Here in the long mountain valleys and high plateaus of the Interior, we haven't missed the boat, and we haven't been asleep. We have been a country.

From Garry Gottfriedson I learned that it is possible still to use those old, problematic words like man, woman, tree, bird, and love, the words of the earth – not as a retreat, not as a suppression of the joys of abstraction and its silences, but as a means of making ourselves fully alive. A cloud shines from ten kilometres deep in the water. A hand dips through it, into the black water of the beginning of the world.

In Toronto, I heard sirens that came from what seemed like twenty miles away: inexorable, sad as loons. Now it is All Saints' Day: a new year. Last night was Hallowe'en. After the kids were asleep, I uncorked a bottle of cabernet, two years old, that Gord and I made in Summerland, and with a glass of wine in one hand and a candle and matches in the other, I walked out into the dark and dug a small hole under the aspens. The toads which used to stare the cats down every summer night on the warm concrete in front of the house, and which hunted flies among the giant zinnias, like the Yanomano on the floor of the rainforest with their blowtubes and their body paint, were asleep in the mud piles right beside me. I wouldn't see them again until the spring, when the air would be as sweet as a glass of water and cool as a trout, in those first days when the loons would return and chase each other screaming around the lake. I was quiet. I let the toads rest.

I set the candle in the bottom of the hole, lit it, then to cut the low wind running just over the grass, ringed it with rocks. The fire flickered and tossed warmly on the aspens. I stood tall above it and took a deep drink of wine. It splashed through my body, like a field of Indian paintbrush caught by a breeze. I shivered. I knew exactly what I had to do. I stood there in the aspen saplings and called all the people of the earth who have touched me, who I have lived with for a brief time, and promised to carry their stories. I poured the rest of my glass of wine around the base of the candle and walked quickly in. The trees shone silver above the black soil, and I knew it was good. The dead were there. They weren't locked in books or in memory. This was their private ceremony, *their* time, like shy animals come in out of the dark. I had no place there, just as I have no place in the forest in the early fall when the bears are hungry and come in and prowl around the horse pens in the moonlight. I went in. Late that night, as we slept in the house, it snowed, covering the burnt-up stub of the candle. I got up in the morning, and a white angel lay over all the land, cold and clean. I called out, "It's winter!"

A week later, the lake froze, without wind and without snow. Day by day during that week I had watched the other lakes freeze – Tatton Lake, Sepa Lake, 105 Lake – but our green and burnished enamel water stayed clear: one last cold drink of the sky. They were cold days. The trees were giving off no more oxygen; the sky was thin. All night the ice that had formed in the shallow black water rimming the shore would break up in the night breeze with the sound of a hundred thousand.faint little crystal bells in the starlight – a breeze so cold and clean it was as if it had just come directly out of the needles of the pines. The coots, as black as seals, paddled around in flocks of thirty, breaking the ice up as it froze around their feet. They hung on to the very end. The water was the colour of cold. It looked blue from a distance, but up close it was black and thick, so black and thick it seemed it wouldn't fall off my fingers when I dipped them in, but it did, slowly and absolutely clearly – the drops hardly different in colour from the air as they fell through it.

Every morning another lake went still and quiet. Then one morning our lake too had left us. It was a sheet of glass. A thin white dust of snow lay on the hills, among the grasses under the trees. Without the tinkling of the bells in the moon-light, the air was strangely quiet. There were no birds, or any other living thing. It was as if we were totally abandoned. A week later, with heavy hoarfrost on the willows rimming the reeds and in the sedges and thistles, the ice was six inches thick. We walked out onto it at five in the afternoon and suddenly gasped, for in that pale, thin evening light that gave a transparency to everything on this drifting earth, the ice was not there under our feet, nor the lake, only the rocks and beaver logs on the bottom, still, covered in a dim, yellow silt. A few blue-white stars and the moon, with a black cancer eating into its face, flashed pale through the veil of the violet air. We walked out slowly over the ice. As we walked, the ice boomed and cracked all around us. Long lightning strokes flashed out across the lake, and the boom followed them, faster than a gunshot, and was echoed by other pings and deep rumblings from far down the water. Every boom and every ping, no matter its point of origin, sounded into the growing night with the whole face of the lake. A boom that was loud to us, just out over the shallows from the reedbed on the north shore, echoed faintly from the south beach; a ping that was as loud there as a seal calling under pack ice was faint to us, like a twig snapping in underbrush. There, as the moon died away above us and more and more stars bloomed in the lilac light – only the light immediately above the tree line was still a pale, hydrangea blue – a sudden black shape swam by under our feet. We followed it – a muskrat! The water beneath us was dark then, and the mud was black, but there, as the moonlight hardly caught on the slick surface of the lake and the stars bloomed crazily, like the patterns of grub-holes in a fallen tree, the muskrat swam, and we followed it, along the curve of the singing water, until the moon went out, and the stars shone above us, on fire.

Epilogue

OCTOBER 1999

Three years after I went to Toronto and saw the city at the end of time and space, I drove eighteen miles into the bush east of McLeese Lake at thirty-five below. The skies were threatening snow. For a week it had been down to forty-five below every night. The snow squealed harshly underfoot like a nail being pried out of an old two-by-four, and the air had gone completely still. Nothing moved. Silence and stillness had taken on a palpable dimension. It was as if there was no distinction between air and thought. For a week, the plateau had been sheltered by a pale, green wall of cold, shimmering in the distant air, while the cities to the south were paralyzed by snow which fell when wet ocean air had struck that wall. I was driving to see Lorne.

I had first met Lorne the previous summer, at an evening poetry reading at the farmers' market in Williams Lake. I had come the hour north from 100 Mile House, through the bunchgrass pastures and stone outcrops along the San Juan River, and he had come the hour south from McLeese Lake. I passed the lumber yards to the south of town, where the timber of the Chilcotin was stacked a hundred feet deep along the rail-line, and Lorne passed the beetle-killed timber of the Chilcotin, stacked a hundred feet deep north of town, along the wood-fired electric plant and its view properties of singlewide mobile homes, wrecking yards, and weeds. Our hosts were a group of college and high-school students and street kids who wanted to make something happen in the summer. I read about Coyote, because this is his country after all. In my poem, Coyote had bought a farm on the edge of the plateau above the cactus and sagebrush of Big Bar, with a view off the plateau to the glaciers of the Coast Mountains, below which the yellow Fraser carried the dirt from clearcuts down to the sea; he had plowed the old pastures, to let the three million lost salmon of the Fraser River free. They swam down the furrows and out into the moonlight. Lorne read a poem he had written twenty years before when he was still living in the Chilcotin, the vast country between the Fraser River and the sea, about standing at a lakeshore and watching the cranes fly north overhead, their cries flooding across the entire sky, filling it, and how he remembered that moment as he was making love to his wife. It had become a symbol to him of their marriage – not a symbol laid down, but one which had risen up through decades of life together and was, one day, suddenly recognized. The young people wrote abstractly about the seductions of politics and love.

As the air chilled and the first stars came out in the purple air, I sought Lorne out. With his wild grey hair and his handlebar moustache, wearing a pair of jeans and a checked workshirt dried on a line, his face and hands with the scrubbed look of a face and hands that are not too often scrubbed, his eyes sparkling, he looked very much like Bill Miner, the train robber and all-round nice guy. I told Lorne that night that if he ever wanted to put together a manuscript of his poems, I would help him do it. I say this to people often, but few people take me up on it, and I didn't think anything more of it.

In late November, however, I got a letter from Lorne, in shaky script – barely readable. Lorne had had a stroke, followed by brain surgery. He had very nearly died. He had lost almost all of the English language, or any other language for that matter, and had to fight to control his hands enough to write what words he had left. He was asking me to put together a manuscript of his poems. The fear of death spilled through every shaky word. I wrote back that I would come and see him.

And so it was that on New Year's Day I was driving into the bush, with a shovel and a sleeping bag in my trunk, in a winter so cold that the winter-hardy crabapple trees in my garden died, and the blackbirds that the neighbour feeds all winter dropped off nightly, so that after two weeks a flock of forty had been reduced to a flock of a dozen. Mile after mile, the snow slipped back past me. I turned off the snow-packed road onto a smaller road, and turned off that onto a smaller one yet, and again, and again, and then there at last were the horses, Lorne's horses, stamping in the snow, their breath rising in clouds as if there were fires within them, as if there were old steam engines in their bellies, damped down. These are not Cariboo horses, so common around 100 Mile House, the kind that take two incomes to support them – first the ten acres in the country, the fences, the four-wheel drive, the snow-clearing equipment just to get in and out to work to support the enterprise, the sheds, the hay, the vet bills, and the moose coming in to eat the hay in the winter, all so you can see the horses with their heads hanging over the peeling white rails of the fence, smelling other horses on the wind, as you drive in and out to town. These were work horses, standing on legs like the pylons of the Hibernia oil platform, moving slowly but with sureness and steadiness, in a meadow two feet deep with snow, under a sun as thin as a sheet of paper. Their size gave such assurance to their movements that they seemed agents of a greater power, a physical power within all of us, made manifest. The snow was a pastel colour, like hydrangeas, glowing from within the snow itself, deepening into violet in the shadows. The driveway was strewn with hay. I parked among even more horses. They towered above the car, hay hanging out of their mouths, and watched me calmly, their deep black eyes twinkling just as Lorne's had done that day back in the summer, but far more slowly.

I stepped out of the car into the steel cold. It had a taste to it of frozen pine pitch, which lent a purity to the air. I stomped through the snow and the dark pines to the house.

Everyone from that meeting in the summer is there, piled into a single-room log cabin with a sleeping loft partitioned by Hudson's Bay Company blankets hanging from stretched clotheslines. Lorne's wife and children are there, too, including his ten-year-old son who is recovering from having his throat slashed by their (late) dog, which turned vicious without warning. Lorne's sixteen-year-old son has just returned from a three-day trip snowboarding in the bush. Lorne's wife Diana laughs. "I never worry about him when he's out in the bush. He can take care of himself. He goes when he wants and he comes back when he wants. When he needs to sleep he cuts himself a snow cave and slips in there for the night." Needless to say, he has dropped out of school. "He found the rules too limiting," says Lorne. "We tried teaching him by correspondence. He does it when he can. He's been working on Grade 10 for two years now. He has a hard time seeing any point to the nonsense."

Diana makes us tea, while Lorne searches for words.

"The whole language part of my brain was destroyed," he says. "The doctors said I'd never recover, but slowly the words are coming back. For instance, I can't remember the word for what happens in a poem when ... you ... say one thing and ... like ... mean something else. What is the ... word ... for that?"

"Metaphor?" I suggest.

"Well, there you go," he says. "Metaphor."

The room is filled with laughter as everyone catches up on a fall spent away, at school, snowboarding around Horsefly, or working with street kids on an outreach pogram in town. In Williams Lake, as in so many places, poetry is not for those who belong.

Lorne takes me aside. "I really appreciate what you're doing for me, man," he says, rummaging in a chest of drawers under the stairway leading up to the sleeping loft. "I don't know how I am going to support the family. I don't have any money. People in McLeese Lake had a dance in the community hall and gave us all the money: $2,000. Just like that. I said, 'You can't do that,' and they told me they sure could and just to take it. That's what we've been living on, but it's nearly gone." He pulls out a big stack of papers – they look like they have been jammed in there one at a time for twenty years. He dumps them on the table, sliding aside a tin of oysters someone brought, and a bottle of wine, and a tray of chips. "I've been typing these things out, but it's terribly slow. I can do one a day, but then my head is all woolly and I'm so exhausted that I have to sleep for a few hours. Then I can work on another poem."

Then he tells me his life story. I help him by filling in the words he has forgotten.

"It's terrible, you know. I can remember people's faces, and remember something we did together, but I can't remember their names. Sometimes I don't remember anything at all, and they have to tell me. Most of what I know now, people had to tell me. Then the memories came back, sometimes, or sometimes I just have to believe them." He laughs.

Lorne went to Simon Fraser University in the sixties, when that Machu Picchu of the temperate rainforest still smelled new and the campus surged with revolution. He finished an undergraduate degree in English and was working on an MA, with a thesis on the poetry of William Carlos Williams. It all came crashing down when he received a Canada Council grant to go to New York and study the Williams archives, to prove his thesis. After three days, he realized that his thesis was bogus, and that all he would be able to do was say how Williams's work did not follow his thesis – and even that would have been a stretch. "It's all so much bullshit," he says. "It's counting laundry tickets. It's just the system." Lorne packed it all in and went drifting. He wound up driving a team of horses for Caravan Theatre in Armstrong. In those first years the performers went from town to town on a large wagon pulled by horses. "It was wonderful to be around all those actors," he says. "It was very creative. I loved it there."

After that, he taught philosophy at Royal Roads Military College in Victoria, and worked as a teacher at Alkali Lake, a reserve town out in the Chilcotin. "Out at Alkali Lake," he says, "they had never had a teacher who wasn't a priest, so that's what they called me, too – Father Lorne. 'Noooo-o-o way,' I told them, but they still called me that. They still do, when I go back. Father Lorne."

When Caravan Theatre gave up on the idea of horses,

Lorne remembered how much he loved them and bought them. He has been horse logging ever since.

He is also a stubborn and very principled man.

Poem by poem, he relives his life for me, trying to nail himself down to the earth he came so close to drifting away from into imprisonment in an ultimate silence. In the pile from his drawer are angry, working-class poems, addressed to the Soviet poet Yevtushenko, contrasting his sell-out to political respectability with the beauty of Lorne's own landscape and the sell-out of horse loggers, working men who just want to live on the earth, to big logging companies, of how the companies and the government work hand-in-hand to keep men like him from work. "Zirnhelt used to be a horse logger, and was one of my friends. Now he's the Minister of Forests and has forgotten where he came from. He should know better. He does know better. I don't know how he sleeps at night." There are the love poems for Diana, ranging from the awkward and purely private to the luminescent. The luminescent ones are all about living in a big caravan tent for eleven years, at fifty and fifty-five below zero, with a woodstove to give them some heat, "just to see what it was like to live on the land as the Indians did." His eyes twinkle. In Lorne's drawer there are poems about his children, an awful lot of poems about snow, and the poems about his horses, about working with his horses, how if you are going to work with horses you are going to have to leave time for dreaming, for if the horses want to stand still for a moment, listening to some hidden music or lost in dreams of running free on the steppes, deep and mysterious as the sea, you won't get them moving again. You're better off to pull out a plug of tobacco, sit down beside the trail, your back to a tree trunk, and roll yourself a cigarette.

The rest of the party recedes as Lorne pulls out poem after poem and slides them to me through the conversation. There are poems about Lorne's childhood in a French town in Northern Ontario, where his father was a horse logger, where winos would sleep under the lilac hedges and a young boy would skip school to talk to them, and they would welcome him among them – laments for a lost culture and a lost language. It can never be returned to, yet it is obvious that Lorne has re-created it here, in the bush eighteen miles east of McLeese Lake, in a cabin he and his wife and their horses built – out of pure idealism and stubbornness. Lorne has been living a poem, for twenty years.

All afternoon it has been snowing. At 7 p.m. there are eight inches of snow on the hood of my car. The protective cold that has sheltered us from the crippling snowstorms that paralyzed the Coast has finally broken. The snow re-forms as quickly as I can sweep it away. I back out among the horses and make my way down the now snowed-in roads towards McLeese Lake. A handful of Lorne's poems lie on the seat beside me. Lorne will send the rest in three weeks. The visibility is no more than fifty yards. The road is scarcely discernible. I am driving through a white world outside of time and space. The highway south to Williams Lake and 100 Mile is even worse. There, the snow is a foot deep and cut up into a myriad of tracks, crisscrossing each other. The visibility is down to ten yards, and slowly I creep south, only occasionally glimpsing the taillights of the car in front of me. On that four-hour drive, I think of Lorne's son, moving confidently out on the land, so capable and sure, and wonder if the land will be able to support him, if Lorne's big gamble will pay off. It's hard to imagine being any closer to the earth, with the stars overhead in the night sky like flecks of foam on the flanks of a blue whale flicking its tail and diving deep, but I have my doubts.

For two years now, Lorne has peddled his manuscript in Vancouver. He is growing depressed. "It's hard," he says. "Look what I've done to my family. I've made them live as they do for twenty years, because of my poetry. I would feel a lot better about it if at least I had a book published. Then I wouldn't feel so guilty, at least. Publishers have been rejecting my book because I don't have a lot of literary magazine publications behind me. They say that without that they won't even look at it. 'Serious poets publish in literary magazines first.' Jesus. The years I have spent at this don't count for anything. I don't know what kind of world they live in, but I have been working, to feed my family. When I come home at night I don't have the energy to send anything away to anyone. Come see me, man."